D1556946

1

The **MINDSET** RETIREMENT

how I
RETIRED
at age **55**
- with no money

Beth Rand

Copyright 2017

Table of Contents

Chapter 1

Introduction

*"If one advances confidently in the direction of his dreams,
and endeavors to live the life which he has imagined,
he will meet with a success unexpected in common hours."*
- Henry David Thoreau

An article caught my eye one day. The title was about how to grow your finances in retirement, and it promised to tell 4 strategies that work! I eagerly turned straight to the page. The strategies? First, meet with your financial advisor to adjust your *retirement funds* according to your current health. Second, review your life insurance policy to see if those *retirement funds* could be put to better use now. Next, have another look at the *retirement funds* in your retirement portfolio and consider reallocating your assets. And finally, assess the equity of your house and consider converting to liquid *retirement funds*.

Are you thinking the same thing I was thinking?

RETIREMENT FUNDS? WHAT RETIREMENT FUNDS?!

If you're in the same situation I'm in, this was your first reaction too! So, chances are you've picked up this book because some, similar, or all, of the following circumstances which apply to me currently apply to you too:

- ✓ You are 10 to 15 years away from a traditional retirement age range.

- ✓ You in a situation where you have very little or no money saved for retirement, and you don't see how you will be able to afford to retire by age 70.

- ✓ You are, or you are soon to be, an Empty Nester.

- ✓ You are too young to be able to claim social security, Medicare, etc, yet you really need it *now*.

- ✓ Anyway, your Social Security check is not likely going to be enough to live on alone.

- ✓ You're unable to find a full time job in your field that pays enough to make ends meet, let alone put aside anything for your retirement years.

- ✓ Or - you may be in that low paying full time job now, but you're not making ends meet, and you're not happy there anyway.

- ✓ You are working one or more intermittent or part time jobs.

- ✓ You are able to get some consultancy work in your field.

- ✓ You have started, or are considering starting, your own business.

- ✓ You are toying with the idea of going back to school.

- ✓ You have, or you plan to get, one or more rental properties, or rent out a part of your own home.

- ✓ You are, or you hope to be, teaching a course; online or at a local community college.

- ✓ You are creative and good with your hands, and you are, or you are you considering, selling your creations; either in person or online?

- ✓ You are, or you have, toyed with the idea of, creating a website that showcases your enterprises, products or services?

✓ You moved, or are thinking of moving, to another part of your town/state/country/world because it has a lower cost of living.

✓ You are, or you are considering, downsizing to a smaller house/townhouse/condo/apartment.

✓ _____ _____

[*fill in your own*].

If you are in any or all of these situations, you may be thinking

this wasn't how I saw my upcoming retirement happening.

You may have always been struggling, or you may have recently lost it all (or too much of it). You may have found yourself in this situation from any variety of paths. It may be because:

✓ you lost your savings, house equity, and/or investments around 2008 because of the recession,

✓ you are, or have been, a divorced single parent (usually women, but not always),

✓ your company downsized, closed, or laid you off because of the recession,

✓ your own business had to be closed because of the recession,

✓ medical reasons have prevented you from physically working,

✓ you've been hit by a serious disaster, natural or otherwise,

✓ _____

[*fill in your own*].

Regardless of how we all came to be in this situation we are not alone. In the April 15, 2009 issue of Time Magazine, in her article about the "The Great Recession" Nancy Gibbs writes of people in this country, that "Nearly half say their economic status declined this year...". She goes on to quote more statistics, such as "...34% have not gone to the doctor because of the cost, 31% have been out of work at some point, and 13% have been hungry." Further statistics reported are: "Forty percent of people at all income levels say they feel anxious, 32% have trouble sleeping, and 20% are depressed." And even though she says that people are feeling "more resolve than regret" she goes on to say that "Even when prosperity returns, 61% predict, they'll continue to spend less than they did before."

An article in the November 2017 issue of Money magazine, titled "Retire Like Suze!" (referring to financial guru, Suze Orman, who has just retired from her TV show) continues the dialog, reporting that "Each year, six in 10 people get hit with a financial shock they can't afford, such as a health crisis, layoff, or major expense that wasn't in their budget...The median working-age family has only $5,000 in its retirement accounts..."

You may be one of these statistics, and perhaps your earning potential is now so low that there is no way that in the remaining 10 to 15 years before the traditional retirement age could you save up enough money to retire. In addition, because you aren't yet of retirement age, you can't even yet rely on any social security or Medicare to supplement your efforts. And now you are wondering how you are ever going to retire at all, because at this point, all you are managing to do is to piece together an existence.

Like many people in this country, you are not alone. My own story is coming up, but in a nutshell - due to a divorce in my late 40's, after being a stay at home mother for nearly two decades, I ended up fresh in the work force with only the equity in my house to my name (but even that didn't last long – my divorce happened just before the recession and I lost all my equity) - and a very low earning potential (more on that later). I did manage to have a few years of employment while I finished raising my children, but we lived at a subsistence level, and I certainly did not make enough money to put aside any retirement savings for myself.

After my youngest left home to go to college, and after I downsized and moved halfway across the country to a place with a lower cost of living, I found myself piecing together an existence; tutoring math, teaching an online course I'd created, freelance designing, and self-publishing a few books.

You have possibly had a similar - albeit unique - path of your own that brought you into a similar financial situation a decade or so before you were due to retire. Many people (usually women, but not always) are in a similar financial state because of divorce. A lot of other people got into this financial state because of the financial crisis that happened around 2008 and have never been able to recover. If you own a home you may have been relying on the equity for your retirement, yet your home value may have yet to return to the pre-mortgage crisis level. You may have experienced a natural disaster, or medical set back. You may be reading this book because you are one of those people. You are not alone in how you are faring and feeling.

DISCLAIMER

This is not a "How To" book, and I'm not a financial expert – although I will have pages of 'advice' – but mostly it's the story of my own journey and a sharing of what actions I took that grew out of my journey, that hopefully will inspire you in your own journey!

I'm not going to address traditional retirement practices, such as investing, government programs, etc. If you're reading this book, you probably, like me, have nothing or little to invest, and you are too young to qualify for social security or Medicare. However, if the opposite is the case for you and you're in good standing that's great, and there are a lot of books and websites out there where you can find traditional retirement and investment advice. (Some ideas can be found in the Resources section at the end of the book.)

The opinions, guidance, conclusions and results expressed in this book are based on my experiences. Your situation may differ from the situations presented here. Always consult financial and legal counsel as necessary regarding your specific case.

I can't tell you what to do or how to do it in your unique life, but like me, you can have a *mindset* of retirement that will help you stop stressing about your *financial* retirement and spur you into the action of retiring *NOW!*

Chapter 2

My Story
(Or: My Paths to my Mindset Retirement)

"How vain it is to sit down to write
when you have not stood up to live."
- Henry David Thoreau

Before we go any further, I would like to share my story with you, because it was from my own story that this book arose.

MY DIVORCE PATH

It all began in 2005, when, two days after I finished two years of schooling to get my teaching certificate, my then husband, father of our two boys and stepfather of my daughter, announced that he wanted out of the marriage. So that was that for me.

I had essentially been a stay at home mother for 28 years. I have three wonderful children, who, as of this writing are ages 28, 22 and 18. I was married twice within that time period to husbands who each traveled for a living while I raised the kids. I had a college degree, and still freelanced – my ex would say 'dabbled' - in my specialty - educational tech theatre.

When we divorced, because we lived in a community property state, we divided our assets in half. At the time, the equity in our home, about $230,000, was closely equal to the amount in my husband's work retirement account. So that seemed like a fair division.

But, it was not equitable at all. Our division of funds did not take into account each of our future earning potentials. He had been

13

climbing the corporate ladder and I had been a stay-at-home mother out of the work force. After the divorce I was no better off financially than a 23 year old fresh out of college (with 3 children) looking for a job and starting on the bottom rung of the teacher pay scale. The state mandated division of funds did not take into account the time involved in raising up our 3 children, which had not left me free to travel or work executive hours in order to raise up the corporate ladder.

According to an article in More Magazine (June 2007) "a mother who is out of the workforce for just three years can lose up to 37% of her earning power". Kathleen Miller, in her book "Fair Share Divorce for Mothers" (a book you cannot do without if you are contemplating a divorce!) states: "Following divorce, mothers typically experience a sharp decline in economic status and often descend into poverty with their children. Nearly 40 percent of divorced mothers are poor." And it's not only in America that we find these inequities. An article from the British newspaper The Guardian's website, titled "Men become richer after divorce" points out research that shows "When a father separates from the mother of his children...his available income increases by around one third. Women, in contrast, suffer severe financial penalties...the incomes of "separating husbands" rise "immediately and continuously" in the years following a marital split". Furthermore, combined results of five surveys in Europe, from the same article "...found that the positive effect on men's finances is so significant that divorce can even lift them out of poverty, while women are far more likely to be plunged into destitution. Separated women have a poverty rate of 27% - almost three times that of their former husbands."

Divorce – or rather the state laws pertaining to how money is allocated at the time of divorce - was how I got into this financial state.

But, it was also a double whammy for me, because the financial crisis happened just as I should have been getting back on my feet after my divorce. In particular, the one asset that I did have – the equity in my house – should have been increasing in value. Instead, the value of my house dropped about $200,000 and had only just recovered to its divorce-time value by the time I sold it 12 years later. I essentially not only lost $200,000, but also 12 years of appreciation.

So while I feel I dodged a bullet and avoided the meaningless (to me) life of an 'executive wife', financially I'd been shot in the wallet. Yes, I was lucky to have good child support and maintenance for a few years (never underestimate the value of a good lawyer!), which allowed my children to stay in our family home and stay in their school district, but there was no money left for any sort of savings. We lived the middle class 'working poor' hand-to-mouth subsistence.

MY CAREER PATH

So how did I survived financially for the remaining 12 years of parenthood after the divorce? The first year of single life was an adjustment for me, and for the kids who had been lucky to have a stay-at-home mother. For the first year alone I could only find work as a substitute teacher in our local school district. In 2006 I managed to get hired for a half time teaching position, but in February of 2007 I was informed that the teacher who had vacated the post wanted his job back. I was contracted to keep teaching until the end of the school year, but I was very discouraged. (It should be mentioned here that when I say "year" I actually mean "school year", because that's the schedule my life revolved around.)

Throughout the summer of 2007 I looked for teaching jobs, but didn't get hired. As I was still receiving maintenance (alimony) I decided that this was a sign that I should start a business, so when my kids went back to school in 2007 my work began in earnest. I've always had an 'entrepreneurial spirit', so I decided to start a consulting business helping other divorced women.

I researched and researched, I planned and planned. I organized and organized. I had a website. I had forms and documents. I had policies and procedures. I'd done my due diligence. When I was ready, in early 2008, I hung out my shingles. And I started to get a few clients. But do you know what – I found that I really didn't like having to repeatedly tap into my own divorce experiences in order to help clients with theirs. I really didn't want a job where I focused on my own divorce for the rest of my life – I wanted to move on.

All was not lost though. Out of all that due diligence arose my book "*Rise Above Your Divorce and Land on Your FEET: Financially secure; Emotionally stable; Efficiently operating; Tomorrow focused*" written under the pseudonym Betty Gordon, necessary at the time. You can still find my book on Amazon. Additional good books on divorce are listed in the Resources section of this book.

So, in the summer of 2008 I put the idea of having a business on the back burner, self-published my book, and started applying for teaching jobs again. I managed to get yet another part time teaching job – and still only a year's contract. As my former classmates and I discovered, it wasn't as easy to get a permanent teaching job as they'd told us it would be in school! Particularly in 2008. At the end of the school year in 2009 that job ended, too.

It was in 2009 that the recession really hit me hard and I was not able to get a job at all that year. Concurrently, my older son was befallen with some major medical issues. So I spent that year mostly being there for my him, taking him to appointments, and advocating for him at school; medically, academically and socially. It was the toughest, scariest year of my life – not to mention how it must have been for my son. It was also the year that my maintenance was due to end. Luckily I had whom I consider to be the *World's Best Lawyer*, who advocated for me in court, where I was awarded an 18-month extension on my maintenance because of the recession. Thankfully my son did eventually pull through – mostly thanks to an awesome school counselor and a wonderful medical practitioner – and is doing just fine, as if it were all just one long nightmare.

That was my "job" that year. I don't know how I could have been working outside of the home during that year – I would have surely lost my job for being absent so much. However, I was not completely cerebrally idle that year. I also did an online course – which left me flexible to help my son – and got my Master's of Science degree. This was completely unplanned and it happened only by sheer, fortuitous chance that I came across the degree program and found that they had a one-year intensive online masters degree program in the field of theatre business management. I applied and by that October had started the course. Doing a Master's degree online in one year was very intense, but it allowed me the flexibility to be there for my son when he needed me.

And it made me more employable as a result. Two days after I graduated in October, 2010 I was hired as a high school Theatre Manager in a neighboring school district. It was still a part time position, paid hourly and with minimal benefits, but it eventually became full time. And while I still received Child Support for the children, my maintenance ended. I stayed at that school district for 5 years, and then moved to another district, again as a Theatre Manager, but in a teacher-salaried position, for another 2 years. (There was no difference in the work I did, it's just that each district classified the position differently.)

But again, that job – on a educator's salary – barely helped make ends meet, and certainly did not afford me the luxury of having any retirement savings. (Yes there was a retirement savings plan at the school districts, but for the period of time I had worked, I accrued only enough to cash in, in order to buy three teenager-cars, because the kids needed to be able to drive themselves to their activities while I was at work, and my ex refused to help out.) The child support, of course, went towards the cost of raising our children.

And despite also having published 7 books in my field, by the time I became an empty nester at age 55 I had no savings. I was lucky to have about $200,000 equity in my townhouse that I owned outright after I downsized, but that would not see me through retirement as I would still need a place to live. Some of you reading this book may not even be in this position.

My earning potential was still low – I was then on tier 4 of the teacher's pay scale, about the same as a 27 year old having taught for 4 years right out of college – so there was no way that between 55 and 70 that I could save up enough to live on for the rest of my life. So I figured I'd be working through my retirement.

MY MINDSET RETIREMENT PATH

Even though I was 'gainfully employed', my entrepreneurial spirit was still alive inside of me. When my youngest son started high school – 4 years before the writing of this book – I just knew that something different had to happen in my life when he left for college. It was during those 4 years that I started to create a high school theatre design and operations consulting business, while still working full time at the school district. I didn't earn much, or sometimes any, money from my business during that time, but I was getting myself known in the national high school theatre community.

It was also during those 4 years that I started 'purging' my house. How do we collect so much *stuff*?! I didn't know what was going to happen to me when I became an Empty Nester, but I knew I needed to get rid of *stuff*. Perhaps I would meet someone who would move in with me – and fill my house with his *stuff*. Perhaps I would renovate the kids' bedrooms and bathroom into a separate apartment and rent it out. Perhaps I would find another part of the country to move to with a lower cost of living. Perhaps I would move into a smaller house. Whatever was going to happen, I knew I would need to trim my possessions.

During that time as I was tinkering in my business and purging my house, I was in contact with a lot of high school theatre teachers and staff around the country. About 2 years into my 4 year journey to who-knows-where, I discovered that Colorado has more support for high school tech theatre, and also has a lower cost of living than the Seattle area. It also had more sun! And more snow! The seed was sewn – I knew what I wanted to do. So, after some research and planning, when my youngest left home to go to college I moved to Colorado. One huge benefit of moving from the Seattle area was a reduction in my cost of living. Admittedly I have a smaller place now, but my property taxes have gone from $7000 a year, to $1200 a year! Not that I minded paying property taxes - my kids needed a house to live in and public schools to go to - but in my situation, that had been a contributing factor of my financial hardship. And, in order to retire at 55, a reduction in expenses was a necessary action to take.

YOUR UNIQUE PATH

So this is where you find me now. I started a new life. My freelance business has begun to take off. I'm not saying you should move across the country, but I'm just sharing what happened to me as an example. Your steps will be different, but I hope that my story may inspire you to see that no matter how you ended up with no retirement savings, no matter your own story, all is not lost! Your money may be lost, but not your resourcefulness, your integrity, your creativity and your positive mindset.

As I said, this is not a "how to" book (although I do offer my ideas and philosophies about what worked for me and what I believe will prove to be useful advice to you). I do hope that through sharing my story, journey and ideas in this book, it will give you inspiration, and help you to start considering your own story. I hope to show you how to adapt your own financial cituation within your own definition of a Mindset Retirement (more on just what this is soon) as best suits you and your life, while staying healthy and happy throughout your own journey. Let's begin.

Chapter 3

The Bog of Retirement

"...stress occurs only when we care about something..."
- Unknown

Spoiler alert - this is the depressing chapter.

Before we look at what a Mindset Retirement is, we're going to begin by looking at how the situation first looked for me, and may look for you right now. But fear not, we will soon climb out of the bog, so read on.

WHAT IS THE RETIREMENT BOG?

When you and I are stuck in the Retirement Bog we are just trying to get by day-to-day. When we are stuck in the Retirement Bog we are fed up of media stories such as: *Martha and George have worked hard towards their higher purpose, and invested soundly in order to build a solid financial plan for their retirement.*

It's not like you haven't been working hard too – in fact you may have been working harder than Martha and George – but for one reason or another (the recession, divorce, lay offs, health, natural disasters, and so on) you currently do not have a 'solid financial plan' for your upcoming retirement.

The stress of your financial situation can leave your emotional and physical health weakened. You're not likely to be concerned about attaining your 'higher purpose', let alone your 'solid financial plan', at this time. You may find yourself desperately swimming just to stay afloat, just to avoid being sucked into the bog, which you never seem to be able to climb out of.

You may begin to wonder what is wrong with you. You may feel depressed, isolated, withdrawn and incompetent, like you're going crazy. You may sometimes feel as if you've lost faith, and as if you are no longer interested in bettering yourself, let alone your finances. You may lose friends because you have to turn down social invitations due to lack of time, energy and money. You may lose job opportunities because you cannot give your all to you work obligations.

When we are stuck in the Retirement Bog, there is little or no time or money left for activities that used to be taken for granted. These become extraneous and laborious. For me these activities included (but are not limited to – depending on your own situation):

Job advancement

> You really should go to that networking dinner this evening after work, but you worked late last night, and you can't really justify the expense anyway.

Volunteering

> You no longer have the time or left-over energy to go to the soup kitchen, and you can't justify sending even $10 a month to your public radio station this year, because you need it yourself.

Social life

> When you have little time, energy or money, you find yourself declining any impromptu "going out for drinks" with friends or after work, or party invitations, and pretty soon you find you have no social life.

Housework and yard work

> You do what you can, when you can, but you can never catch up.

Creativity

> You just can't justify spending the time and money on hobbies and/or classes, when there is so much else that really needs to get done.

Health

> You're concerned about that mole you've been keeping an eye on, that dull pain in your chest concerns you, you wonder if your constant headaches are a sign of something more, you really are overdue for your teeth cleaning, but not only do you not have the time (you're probably ok...), you don't even have the money to spare for your co-pay (assuming you even have good insurance).

Exercise

> The last thing you want to do when you've been going all day is to go any further. Anyway, *Important Things* crop up. If you do have any energy left, time spent on exercise feels selfish and therefore a low priority. That's if you can justify putting money towards exercise at all.

Diet

> Let's face it, no matter what diet you try, it's essentially calories in verses calories out. And that means, in order to lose weight, or even to maintain your weight (especially once you're over 40!) you have to be at least a bit hungry at least a part of each day. It's very hard to be hungry for food, when you are hungry for money and time. It's just one more thing that you are deprived of.

FINANCES IN THE BOG

You may already be living at a subsistence level, and you can't see how you can consider building savings and investments for your retirement, on top of everything you have to cope with. Either the money just doesn't exist, or you are so bogged down with trying to make ends meet for the rest of your lifetime, that you don't have time to raise your head out of the Retirement Bog to even research and schedule a meeting with a financial advisor, let alone take the time off work to attend any meetings or classes.

Conventional wisdom states that the sooner you start investing for your retirement the exponentially better off you will be. But, most of the time the best you can do is to take control of your current budget, and spending, and time.

Even if you do manage to find a bit of money to invest, in an emotional and/or worn out state you might inadvertently cost yourself assets. Finances can be very erratic in the Retirement Bog and you should take your time before deciding on investment decisions. Someone in the Retirement Bog even needs to be careful of utilizing automatic deduction programs, as unpredictable finances can mean a lot of bounced payments, costing you more money and jeopardizing your credit score.

MASLOW'S HIERARCHY OF NEEDS

In 1943 a psychologist by the name of Abraham Maslow wrote, in a paper entitled "A Theory of Human Motivation", that humans have certain needs that are innate, and that some needs are felt more powerfully and are more necessary to survival than others. Not only that, but, most importantly, he maintained that until certain levels of needs are met, a person finds it hard, or sometimes simply unnecessary, to concentrate on the next level. This is the plight of being stuck in the Retirement Bog.

Maslow arranged these needs of life into five categories in a pyramid shaped chart, which he called the "Hierarchy of Needs". The attainment of each level supports the potential to then gain the level above it. Without the supporting levels, the pyramid - or one's life - crumbles. (The hierarchy chart is normally shown with Level 1 being at the bottom and Level 5 being at the top, but is listed here in numerical order.)

Level 1: Biological and Physiological Needs

At the base of the pyramid are the physiological and biological needs for air, food and water, sleep, and shelter. Without these needs being met the body cannot physically function. Also, without these needs being met,

24

empathy for others is hard to attain in the struggle just to survive.

Level 2: Safety Needs

Once biological and physiological needs are met, we then begin to be concerned with safety, protection, family, societal organization and stability.

Level 3: Belongingness and Love Needs

After the physical needs in levels one and two are met, we begin to yearn for social needs such as, love, companionship (in the form of friends, family, work groups, etc.) and collaboration. At this point we are also able to give to others. If these needs are not met, people can become depressed, anxious and lonely.

Level 4: Esteem Needs

This is the level where a person can not only attain achievement, status and reputation, but also the healthy basic needs to be respected by others and to respect yourself, which usually result in a healthy self-esteem.

Level 5: Self-actualization

The fifth level includes self-actualization and personal growth. In this day and age this level might positively be referred to as "self-confidence" and in its negative manifestation is referred to as narcissism. However it manifests itself, the need for self-actualization can only be met once the lower level needs have been satisfied.

Maslow considered the bottom two levels as "self-oriented needs", while the top three levels are "other focused needs". The bottom two levels may also include looking after others, but if they are, then they usually seem to be in the way of service and protection of others not in the way of return on investment. The top three ('other' oriented) levels can manifest in a positive altruistic way, or in a negative "notice me" way usually reserved for those with narcissistic tendencies.

Maslow considered the fifth level as a "Growth Need". When the growth needs are fulfilled, they can enhance an already good and stable psyche. But a person can live without these needs and still feel fulfilled, safe and loved. You can, and maybe do, exist without these higher needs being met at this time.

Maslow called the bottom four levels "Deficiency Needs". The fulfillment of these needs can be taken for granted by a person with enough money. A person doesn't really notice them as "needs", unless they are absent, at which point the deficiency creates anxiety and tension. It's at the point when we realize we are deficient of enough money to retire on that this emotional deficiency is heightened.

People in war-torn countries, the homeless, some impoverished primitive societies, and the 'working poor' are usually stuck at one of the three lower levels.

The fourth and fifth levels are not so imperative for our physical survival, but can make the difference between being alive and living life. The fourth level (Esteem Needs) can be the hardest to lose when you are in the situation of not having enough for your retirement. The top level may be missed, but losing the 4th level can cut you to the core.

Towards the end of his life, Abraham Maslow recognized that a sixth "Self-transcendence" level existed, where the individual was in a realm where illumination and insights changed their view of the world and of themselves.

In today's world one example is a woman called Nani Ma, living in India, who was described as an "enlightened Saint" in the book *The Passion Test*, by Janet Bray Attwood and Chris Attwood. This woman was originally from England, but had given up her life there after her children were grown, to live in India in a life of "total service" and was "absorbed in the study of deep meditation". She is described as having become the "embodiment of pure knowledge and love." When asked by the authors of this book how one can evoke the laws of attraction and create a wonderful life, Nani Ma had this to say: "The way to create whatever you want in life is by giving it to other people." She goes on to say that "...people think they want money...but nobody really wants anything except happiness." She also talks about serving others as a way to spiritual enlightenment: "When we serve other people we forget ourselves...And the misery of life is when we are lost in ourselves, meaning our egos." Nani Ma also proclaims that "...people who are happy in themselves serve because there is nothing else to do," and that "They are already close to God."

Many "everyday" people are fascinated by the laws of attraction and may have had several such experiences in their lives, myself included. Many people advocate that a positive attitude and outlook will have positive results. Many people believe if they give of themselves selflessly, they will receive abundance in return. Many people work to attain the fifth and sixth levels whenever they can. And many people agree with everything that most enlightened modern-day saints, prophets and spiritualists say.

So, it is at Maslow's sixth level, where if we don't have enough money saved up for retirement, we can feel we are spiritual failures.

But think. "Saints" and "gurus" already have all of their needs met for them. This sixth level can only be met when the five others below have been met. Even spiritual gurus who have given up their "worldly lives" (usually meaning: Western Civilization), have all five of the lower levels of need fulfilled, usually by other people, and sometimes by living off previously earned money. Some live in communes, abbeys, close-knit societies, many with novitiates of some sort "paying their dues" by their service to the more enlightened. The spiritual person's biological and physiological needs, and even their belonging, love and esteem needs are being met because they either live surrounded by a 'family' or by a society which supports their lives in material ways (providing food, shelter, and so on).

This means that people like Nani Ma already had these basic needs met before they could attain the sixth level. They hadn't lost all their money in a recession, in a health crisis, or in the case of a natural disaster, and they weren't having to figure out how to obtain enough money at the time they were attaining that 6th level. They were fed, they were financially secure, they had somewhere to live, they were relatively safe, they led organized and structured lives, they felt belonging and love from the people around them, they attained status and reputation, and what's more they knew they would never "retire" and that they would always be revered and taken care of as they continued to work throughout their later years. And because of all this support of the lower levels of the pyramid, they were therefore able to attain spiritual self-actualization.

Individuals who do not have enough saved up for retirement can put themselves on a guilt trip, thinking that they are not good enough people, thinking that they have lost the grace of God or the Universe because they are not enlightened, feeling selfish because they no longer donate to charity or volunteer, feeling that they are being egotistical if they are not giving enough to other people. But this just isn't true.

Where you are on the Hierarchy of Needs is not because you are a bad, unenlightened person. The 'working poor' subsist on a low income, and need to make the next rent payment. It seems that there's no way the 'working poor' can focus their time on being enlightened if they don't have enough – or any - money saved up to retire (or enter a spiritual community). You can be distracted with, and focused on, trying to survive today; stuck in the Bog of Retirement at Maslow's lower levels. You may feel that you are swimming and swimming in the bog and are unable to get a grasp in order to climb out.

But...no matter how you ended up in the Retirement Bog, you obviously have a desire to get out the bog if you've started reading this book! So now that we've had a good look at life in the bog let's look at what we can do about the situation.

Chapter 4

Retire NOW

*"It's never too late – never too late
to start over, never too late to be happy."*
- Jane Fonda

ESCAPING THE BOG

If you don't have enough money to retire and are living day to day, it's likely that you are struggling in the Retirement Bog and don't know how to get out. There is a way. But the answer may not be in climbing out of the bog. There is no going back and changing the past; when we fell into the bog in the first place. So, the answer lies in escaping the unpleasantness by cleaning up the bog and creating a beautiful, serene swimming hole with a sandy beach.

If you're reading this book, it's most likely because you are in a bad financial situation. But, if you are reading this book, and others like it, it's probably because you are also a proactive person, who believes in cleaning up the bog you are in and empowering yourself towards a better future.

And if this proactive spirit is your modus operandi in life, it's likely that even if you had millions saved for your retirement you wouldn't be a person who plans to idle on a beach all day, knit or incessantly play golf. Even Suze Orman who recently retired at age 66 and is currently spending her life fishing (according to an article in the November 2017 issue of Money magazine) would still "...love to do more, like a series of seminars..." for instance. In fact, an article in the October 2017 issue of Money Magazine stated that even "...affluent pre-retirees were more concerned about not having a regular schedule (64%) than they were not having a regular paycheck (36%), and more than a third said they were worried about how they'll fill their free time and about losing their sense of purpose in life." It goes on to ask if the reader has considered taking steps to make their retired life meaningful and fulfilling by engaging themselves in a new "venture".

If this is your nature too, then it's likely that you are a person who would still want to have your hand in some "venture" during your retirement, regardless of your financial situation; be it teaching, consulting, writing, creating a small business, getting a part time job, making a difference to someone else's life, and so on.

If you're reading this book, while you may like to relax in your retirement at times, I suspect you too have the spirit of character to find new ventures at this time in your life. It just may not feel like it right now from your view in the bog. But read on...

RETIREMENT ROLE MODELS

If you are the enterprising type, you may know, or know of, others who are like-minded. Who are your role models when it comes to enterprising people our age?

Many people can be role models, but their stories remain private, so we may never know about them. So let's look at people we do know about; actors and politicians and other public figures? Some of them didn't even start to succeed until they were in their 50's and 60s. And many of them are still going at 70, 80, even 90. Prince Phillip of England retired at age 95! Mavis Staples, the soul singer and civil rights activist is almost 80 (in 2017) and according to the November 20, 2017 Time magazine issue is not ready to retire. What about Nobel Prize winners? There are many college professors still teaching beyond retirement too. And it's certainly not because these people can't afford to retire.

For myself, my own parents are my greatest role models. At the writing of this book my mother is 84, and still has showings of her award-winning photography. My father, a physicist who is 82, is still consulting for the firm he worked for during his career, inventing new ways to help beat cancer. He has also extensively researched our family tree, back to the 1500's. They both still enjoy camping in their camper van, and even went on a 10-day camping trip to view the 2017 eclipse.

Another role model I have is a woman who didn't start working until she was 47. Admittedly she was still married at the time she went back to work and was supported by her husband, but her story is nonetheless inspirational to me, being abruptly thrown into a retirement situation I didn't expect around the same age.

This woman had been a stay-at-home mother and raised five children. She was essentially out of the work force for about 20 years, as was I. This isn't to say she was idle– according to several sources she did a lot of 'dabbling' and volunteer work; stuffing envelopes for local organizations, baking cookies, driving the car pool, sewing costumes, and even picketing for causes she believed in. She eventually became a chairwoman of a local political organization and would bring her still-school-aged kids along with her to meetings. In 1987 she ran for congress and won, and was later elected as a Speaker of the House. This woman's name is Nancy Pelosi. At the writing of this book she is 77 years old and is the Minority Leader of the United States House of Representatives. And she still doesn't show any signs of only wanting to sit around and knit and play endless games of golf!

In fact, the October 23, 2017 issue of Time magazine reports that "...the average ages in the House and Senate...today they're 59 and 62...including California's Dianne Feinstein, who recently announced that she'll run for re-election at 84."

Just recently, as of this writing, the November 2017 AARP Bulletin newspaper had an article about recent Nobel Prize winner, where it stated that "...nine of the 10 Nobel winners in science or economics this year were over 70, with the youngest being...68". The article goes on to say "...in most cases they made important refinements well past age 50. This year's winners were no fluke. It appears that genius-level work is happening later in life much more often."

Publications are full of these examples of people who aren't just knitting and playing golf after age 65. The October 2017 AARP Bulletin had just highlighted a "preeminent neuroscientist" who's advice is "Play to your strengths – something that challenges you a bit." Brenda Miller is still doing just that in her continuing ground breaking brain research. She is 99.

You may or may not be recognized by AARP or care to run for office, but if you're reading this book I suspect you have the same fortitude as these people. You are not alone in your entrepreneurial spirit that will carry you through an active retirement, regardless of your financial situation.

I even had the honor of working with such a brilliant and inspiring person myself. This woman was a chorographer who ran a dance school that rented the high school theatre I managed at the time. She would wear a cute outfit of capri pants and a denim jacket with sparkles in the back. She would stand up for 5 hours at a time during tech rehearsals, making sure everyone got everything just right. She had raised 5 boys. And you may guess at her age when I tell you she had been a Radio City Music Hall Rockette. She was 89 at the time I worked with her. I told her she was my role model, and that I hoped I would still be running a business and working in the theatre at 89!

Do you have role models like this in your life – either that you know personally, or a public figure whom you admire? Even if you were financially secure, like these people – and baring a major illness or disability (more on that later) - what would you want to do in your retirement? I suspect, if you are the type of person who is reading books like this in order to better your retirement years, that you certainly don't want to sit around and twiddle your thumbs. Have you ever found yourself thinking: if they can have an active, meaningful retirement, so can I!

WHAT DOES RETIREMENT LOOK LIKE

For myself, I don't *need* fancy hotels and resorts. I also don't *need* a house that is fully automated. And I don't *need* a car that goes way faster than the speed limit. I don't *need* a camera in my refrigerator. I don't *need* to stand on a hoverboard in my living room. I don't *need* a wristband that takes my pulse. I don't *need* an invisible friend named Alexa. I mean, when is enough enough? But I do need to be occupied in worthwhile endeavors, and I do expect to have an active, meaningful retirement. So, I began to think to myself - *let's forget your financial situation just for a moment, and imagine you were financially set for your retirement, and ask yourself this question:*

What does retirement look like to me?

To me first and foremost retirement looks like:

- ✓ Never again working a permanent full time job that would preclude me from accepting a variety of interesting and meaningful intermittent work.

- ✓ Being an Empty Nester.

Given those specifications, it also looks like:

- ✓ Consulting - like my father.

- ✓ Being creative - like my mother.

- ✓ Building my own consulting and design business.

- ✓ Working one or more intermittent part time jobs.

- ✓ Being an online instructor.

- ✓ Teaching a course at a local college.

- ✓ Tutoring.

- ✓ Possibly going back to school myself.

- ✓ Writing.

- ✓ Having a website that showcases my enterprises.

- ✓ Moving to another part of the country with a lower cost of living.

- ✓ Downsizing from my 4-bedroom home on an acre of land to a nice little townhouse.

Does this list look familiar to you? (If not, review the first list of my circumstances in the Introduction.) This list looked awfully familiar to me! And then it dawned on me:

How will my retirement be any different from my current circumstances?!

I was already acting retired!

A MINDSET RETIREMENT

And once I realized I was already *acting* retired, it was easy to step into starting to *feel* retired.

And from stepping into *feeling* retired, there it was another step to do - *declaring* I was retired.

There is a lot of power in words, and in declarations in particular. If no one had declared 'we are going to the moon', we would not have built a rocket that could fly to the moon. So since I realized that my retirement would be nothing different than what I was doing now, I decide to declare myself:

Retired at 55!

And it was then that my life started to become much more fun, less stressful and more meaningful, and I began to clean up my bog. It wasn't because I was in a *financial* retirement, it was because I was in a *mindset* retirement - NOW.

You can be too.

Of course, it's no good just declaring something. The final step is to be in action about your declaration. You have to pro-actively clean up your bog. The rest of this book is designed to inspire you to not only clean up your bog and turn it into a beautiful, fun watering hole, but to start building your own rocket on your sandy shores.

Start NOW.

Chapter 5

Retirement Finances In Action

"Wealth consists not in having great possessions,
but in having few wants."
- Epictetus

As I've mentioned, declarations can be very powerful, and can change your mindset, which can change your life. But there will be no enduring change without action.

If you've got to the point where you're reading this book you've already likely declared that it's time for you to go to the moon. But the question you are likely asking is, what actions do I need to take in order to build my rocket?

In the moon analogy, the concept of going to the moon wouldn't have happened if no one had declared it in the first place. But unless someone took action to start building the rocket, no one would have gone to the moon at all. The next chapters will give you ideas about how to be in action
- ✓ financially,
- ✓ emotionally,
- ✓ and practically.

The first thing I realized I needed to do was to understand my finances and how much money I really needed to spend. So, the first action I needed to do was to take a hard look at my life and get my finances in order.

There's an old saying that money doesn't buy happiness. Yet not having enough money, and/or spending too much money, are the roots at the bottom of the Retirement Bog. But, without money (or some sort of trade system) one cannot even attain

Maslow's first level of Biological and Physiological needs. If those needs aren't met, the innate human needs above them cannot be met. You do need to find a way to fulfill those first two levels of Maslow's pyramid, yet you also have to look at what your needs really are.

Those who continue to simply "cope" in the Retirement Bog have a right to thrive in their new lives; to clean up their bog, and to emerge into a better life and a secure retirement. It is Maslow's second level that is actually the most important level of our Mindset Retirement, and by focusing on fulfilling the second level, it not only creates a basis from which the other needs above it can grow, but will enhance and better the biological needs in the level below it. It is imperative that you begin to stabilize yourself at a financial, practical and emotional level.

This may seem like the financial "advice" section of the book, but really it's an accounting of the journey of practical steps I took in building my own financial rocket. Your situation may differ, but use these ideas as catalysts to create what will work for you. But remember – don't take my word for it – always check with a financial professional.

The forms and samples in this section will assist you in making home finance decisions that suit your individual situation. We will also look at how to create a budget, so that you can see where your money is going every month, how much expendable income you have after all the household bills are paid, and how to not spend more than you have allotted in any one category. Also in this section, I will show you how to create your own personalized budget spreadsheet.

Finally, I will address the importance of always knowing how much money you have at any given time, and for those of you who haven't done it before, I provide step-by-step instructions on how to balance your check book, with a mock-up bank statement and a mock-up check register for you to practice with.

What this book does not address is long term savings programs, retirement, credit reports, investments, etc. Because, chances are, if you are reading this book, savings and investments may seem like an impossible dream at this point. There are a lot of good books on the market about all those topics, but the most important thing for you to do right now is to get your household finances in order as soon as possible, because that's likely all you have to work with at this time. Then you can go and find all those other books.

So let's be in action.

FROM SCARCITY TO SUFFICIENCY

I immediately found that it was imperative that I focus on reducing my home finances as soon as I could. You don't have to move across the country like I did, and perhaps you already do own or rent in a smaller house in an area with a lower cost of living, but the point I want to get across is that you in order to declare yourself retired now, you not only have to change your mindset, but you will then have to take actions to lower your expenses in some way.

You may be asking me, how can I possibly lower my expenses, I live hand to mouth as it is. But I will ask you to consider what you really have and ask yourself: ***when will it be enough?*** I recently met a working married couple at a dinner, who, in the course of the conversation, revealed in several ways that they were clearly financially comfortable. When they asked me what I did, I mentioned that I consulted, but that I was retired. They looked at me with green faces for a moment, and then collectively rolled their eyes and wished they could be in such a position to have enough funds to retire. It wasn't the moment, but I would have liked to have asked them about their real financial situation, because I could have easily retired on what they already had now. But they clearly didn't see it as 'enough'.

I get it. I was once trapped in the same money situation. Before my divorce my ex was earning a good middle class salary, but it never seemed to cover expenses. After the divorce I somehow managed to raise three happy children on about a quarter of that salary. And, I was happier after the divorce than before the divorce. My ex went on to climb the corporate ladder and become very materialistic, and all I could think was how glad I was that I dodged that bullet, and was not living the '*never enough*', keep up with the Joneses, lifestyle.

If you were once used to going out and purchasing $300.00 purses from Nieman Marcus, think Target from now on (really – they have nice stuff...). One of the hardest things to do is to start having to make judgment calls about how much you really *need* or *want* a given item. Or, if you were used to purchasing everything you thought of that you needed the moment you thought of it (after all, this item only costs $20, and this item only costs $8 and this item only costs $35...), you will soon find that all of these little costs add up really quickly.

For myself, I had to declare a complete moratorium on spending at first. I could easily justify this purchase or that purchase at the time, but they added up quickly. So for many months – almost a year, I purchased only food, gas and vet's bills. No clothes, no shoes, no home decorations, no more lattes. After a long time, I came to recognize what was a *needed* purchase and what was a *wanted* purchase.

It's going to be a shock to the system to have to cut down on thoughtless purchases, but you can get through it with the help of your budget. Even if you didn't particularly have much money, chances are that your financial situation is still about to get tighter, and it's imperative that you always keep constant vigilance. Later on, when your innovative retirement mindset proves fruitful, you can reconsider your financial situation.

But ask yourself this - would you rather be working 8:00am to 6:00pm, day in and day out, *towards* your retirement, or would you rather consider yourself *already* retired and already be working on the financial ventures you enjoy working on. If your mindset is the latter, then your actions need to substantiate your mindset.

MONTHLY BUDGET

No matter your level of finances, it's time for you to create a new budget. There are a lot of computer programs out there to help you with your budget. They include (in alphabetical order), but certainly are not limited to:

Home Finance
Kiplinger's Simply Money
Managing Your Money
Microsoft Money
Quicken
Wealthbuilder

But, I found it was best to custom design my own budget tool at first until I developed a level of familiarity with my financial situation, and was able to decide which program would best suit my needs. In order to get your personal situation under control and understand where you stand, you can use a budget of your own personal design, or one of the mass-produced computer programs.

I found it was best to create my budget on Excel. Besides the fact that Excel keeps everything in nice straight lines for you, it also can perform your calculations for you. So, if an item in your budget increases or decreases you can just enter the new amount, and when Excel immediately calculates your new total you can immediately see what a difference this will make to your total expenses, and perhaps adjust your budget in another area in order to compensate.

Regardless of the program I used, I found there are four categories that I needed to divide my expenses into: fixed, discretionary, variable and frequency.

FIXED EXPENSES

These are expenses that you cannot change and that remain fairly constant month in and month out. Your rent or mortgage, utilities, insurance, child care for work, groceries, gas or bus fares, any debt payments, and so on. You will recognize this as fulfilling the first two levels of Maslow's Hierarchy of Needs; Biological and Physiological Needs, and Safety Needs. What that means is, that if you really had to, you could live within this part of your budget.

DISCRETIONARY EXPENSES

These are the expenses that you decide you can afford if there is any money left over from paying the fixed expenses. These are not vitally important, but are what make your life more bearable and help you value yourself as socially acceptable. While I'm not advocating uncontrolled spending, be reasonable at first. These cover Maslow's next two levels Belongingness and Love Needs, and Esteem Needs, and these needs are also important to your sense of well-being. They include a bit of spending money, lunch money, eating out expenses, activities and exercise, and savings.

You must decide for yourself which expenses you consider as fixed expenses or as discretionary expenses; what is cable TV and Internet for instance? Some people consider contributing to savings as a fixed expense. While I'm not saying don't save, please note that debt payments are included in fixed expenses. If you are paying 18% credit card debt, it's better to put money towards paying that off than towards a 2% savings account or 5% investment. And sometimes until your finances settle down into a consistent pattern you may need every penny you have.

Week's Petty Cash

One way of helping control your spending while allowing yourself a bit of 'sanity money' is to utilize a Weekly Petty Cash system. Although hardly anyone seems to use cash these days, this is a system that worked really well to help me budget some of my money. The Weekly Petty Cash can include an allowance for yourself (unnecessary new clothes, etc.), perhaps a fee you have to pay for an activity, treats and fast food, whatever your situation dictates. Here's how it works. Decide on an amount you can afford to put into the Petty Cash each week. When you pay your bills write out 4 (or 5) checks each dated for each Monday (or day of your choice) in the upcoming month. Each Monday (or whenever) drive through the bank and cash that week's check. Then, once the money is gone, it's gone, and you don't get any more for the rest of that week. This system worked out far better for me than doling myself out spending money monthly, because in that situation it's more tempting to spend it all at once, and then more tempting to let yourself have more because you can't wait another two or three weeks until the next month. It also works better than simply setting aside an amount you allow yourself to spend or withdraw at the ATM, because those are too easy to justify withdrawing a little extra each time. (Because those "each times" add up quickly.) Somehow the physical presence of some cash is a good way to see when it's gone, it's gone. If you have a larger expense, with this system, you can put aside a bit of your week's petty cash each week in an envelope in a drawer, until you've saved up enough for the larger expense.

And here's a little trick for dealing with the Weekly Petty Cash check at the bank. Assuming that every week your needs are the same (a certain allowance amount for each member of the household, an activity fee, and so on) and because you have to divvy up the money between two or more family members, get a blank envelope and write on it the denominations of the bills that you need, and how many of each. Slip the check into the envelope, and hand it to the bank teller, or put it through the drive-through. The teller can then give you your money in the denominations that you need, without you having to reinvent the wheel each week by having to figure it out all over again and having to tell the teller what you need. The tellers at my bank were quite used to me putting my little envelope and check in the drive up window every Monday. Make sure to write on the envelope "Please return this envelope" and make sure it comes back each time with your cash so that you can use it again. This may seem like a lot of work in this day and age of internet payments and phone deposits - it is my hope that one day they'll be able to make cash dispense out of cell phones...! - but in the meantime, the physical act of spending cash still wins out for creating awareness about the budget.

VARIABLE EXPENSES

But what about car and household repair and maintenance, and other large expenses, I hear you ask. Yes, these can be considered necessary expenses, but because they vary each month, put them under a Variable Expenses category, otherwise known as the "There's Always Something" category. These expenses should in fact take precedence over the Discretionary Expenses, and you can organize your spreadsheet as such if you'd prefer, but they're at the end of the list here merely because of their variable nature.

Besides car and house, variable expenses can include uninsured medical bills, vet bills, seasonal or work clothes, gifts, professional services (whether it's the plumber who needs to be called in, or lawyers bills that need to be paid), and so on, and so on, and so on. This list may be never ending, and it's always something different every month, but over time the total Variable Expenses seem to even out. Keep track of your variable expenses for a year, and then use the monthly average as the figure to put into your budget. But remember, if you don't spend all that money one month, you don't get to spend it on other things. It's only an average, which means that some months the amount needed will be higher than others, so you need to keep the money slated for times to come.

41

What about eating out?

Sometimes it really is hard to find the time and energy to shop for and fix a meal and clean up afterwards, and eating out seems like an easy solution. That's fine if you have the funds to do so. The expense may be worth the lowered stress and fatigue level to you. You can decide where to put eating out in your budget. In the example below fast food is included in the week's petty cash, and when that money has run out, the family cannot eat out for the rest of that week. Sit-down restaurants are included in the Variable Expenses because they can be afforded only intermittently. (Nutritional advice is beyond the scope of this book).

FREQUENCY OF EXPENSES

The final category is frequency – how often do you need to pay your bills. Are some due on the first and some due around mid-month, or can you set it up to pay them all once a month? This sample budget is set up to pay bills at the beginning and the middle of the month. You can set up your budget to suit your needs. I don't recommend paying the bills as they come in, however, because it makes it much more difficult to keep track, and to know when you need to cut back before it's too late.

MONTHLY BUDGET BLANK SAMPLE

Following is a sample budget done on an Excel spreadsheet. Note that the numbers do not reflect an actual budget; they were just put in there randomly, and in small amounts, to show you how the automatic totaling works.

	A	B	C	D	E	F
1		MONTHLY BUDGET for _____			(Revised xx/xx/xxxx)	
2						
3		**BEG. MO. BILLS - FIXED**			**MID. MO. BILLS - FIXED**	
4						
5		MORTGAGE/RENT	4		HEALTH INSURANCE	0
6		CAR PAYMENT	0		UNINSURED MEDICAL	0
7		CAR INS.	0		WATER	0
8		INTERNET	0		GARBAGE	0
9		CELL PHONE SERVICE	0		GROCERIES	0
10		ELECTRICITY	0		GAS & BUS FARE	0
11		GAS	0		DEBT/CREDIT PAYMENT	2
12						
13		SUB-TOTAL - BEG.MO.FIXED	4		SUB-TOTAL - MID.MO. FIXED	2
14						
15		**BEG. MO. BILLS - DISCRETIONARY**			**MID. MO. BILLS - DISCRETIONARY**	
16						
17		TV - CABLE	0		LANDLINE PHONE SERVICE	0
18		VIDEO STREAMING SERVICES	0		CHARITY DONATION	0
19		WORK LUNCHES	4		WORK CLOTHES	5
20		4 WK'S PETTY CASH (from below)	12		EXERCISE - CLASSES/GYM	0
21		DVD RENTALS	0		EXTRA DEBT/CREDIT PAYMENT	0
22		OTHER	0		SAVINGS/INVESTMENT	0
23						
24		SUB-TOTAL- BEG.MO.DISCRET.	16		SUB-TOTAL-MID.MO.DISCRET.	5
25						
26		**BEG. MO. BILLS - VARIABLE**			**MID. MO. BILLS - VARIABLE**	
27						
28		**THERE'S ALWAYS SOMETHING**	1		**THERE'S ALWAYS SOMETHING**	3
29		(house repr.&maint., car repr.&maint.,			(house repr.&maint., car repr.&maint.,	
30		uninsured medical co-pays, vet,			uninsured medical co-pays, vet,	
31		clothes, gifts, restaurants, movies			clothes, gifts, restaurants, movies	
32		prof fees, the unexpected ...)			prof fees, the unexpected ...)	
33						
34		SUB-TOTAL- BEG.MO. VARIABLE	1		SUB-TOTAL- BEG.MO.VARIAB	3
35						
36		SUB-TOTAL BEG. MO.	21		SUB-TOTAL MID. MO.	10
37						
38		**MONTHLY BILLS TOTAL**	31			
39						
40		**INCOME**			*** WEEK'S PETTY CASH**	
41		PART TIME JOB	20		PLAY CLOTHING FUND	1
42		FREELANCING	5		MY 'NO GUILT' MONEY	1
43		BOOK ROYALITES	5		FAST FOOD	1
44		OTHER	2		TOTAL WEEK'S PETTY CASH	3
45		**TOTAL INCOME**	32		4 weeks/month	12
46						

EXCEL CALCULATION COMMANDS FOR BUDGET

If you are familiar with excel spreadsheets it will be fairly straightforward for you to set up your own personal budget following a layout similar to this. If not, following is a list of the most common commands that you will need to make up your own personalized budget spreadsheet.

Adding Amounts

=SUM(C5,C6,C7,C8,C9,C10,C11)
or
=SUM(C5:C11)

This command is for when you wish to add some amounts together. For instance, as shown here, in cell C13, you wish to find the total of adding the amounts of the mortgage/rent, car payment, car insurance, internet, cell phone, electricity and gas.

43

If you type either of the above commands in cell C13, it will automatically add up those amounts for you. Then if you change one of those amounts, the new total will automatically occur in cell C13.

Subtracting Amounts

=C10-C9

In this case, we wish to subtract a number in cell C9 from a number in cell C10.

Multiplying Amounts

To multiply a number in cell D2 with a number in cell F10:

=D2*F10

To multiply a number in cell F42 times 4:

=F42*4

Dividing Amounts

To divide a number in A2 by a number in A3:

=A2/A3

Copying or Repeating an Amount

=F45

For example, in the bottom right hand corner of the spreadsheet the Week's Petty Cash has been broken down into the various uses for the money. Once you've figured out how much the total amount of the week's petty cash will be, you want to plug it into your budget. Therefore, in cell C20 you would write the formula above, which tells the spreadsheet to automatically copy the same number from once cell to another. If anything changes in the week's petty cash - changing that number changes the total amount, which automatically is changed in the budget as well.

44

<u>To Keep a Running Total</u>

An example of this can be seen in the Check Book Register mock-up below. Once you have entered in two or more entries in your amounts column and in your balance column, click on the final balance box (cell) that you have. You will see a little box at the bottom right hand corner of the cell. When you hover your curser over this little box, your curser will turn into a plus sign, then drag your curser down the cells in the column as far as you will need (you can always repeat this and add more cells later). Thereafter, each time you add or subtract a number in the amounts column, it will automatically figure the new balance in the balance column.

For other calculations, you can usually find an explanation in Excel's Help menu. There are also a lot of books and free tutorials available that will help you learn how to use Excel.

CREDIT CARD PAY-OFF PLAN

If you're like me, you may be beginning your retirement with at least some credit cards to pay off. It's imperative that you get your finances in order and have a plan to pay off your debts.

But first - don't beat yourself up about debt. For whatever reason, it happened. It's time to stop living in your stories of how it happened and why it happened. Because the whys and the hows aren't going to change the situation now. So, end that conversation in your head and replace it with another conversation – making a plan to pay it off. This is the action section of the book. You have declared yourself retired, and now it's time to take the actions that support that declaration.

Some financial professionals or celebrities advise paying off the card with the highest interest rate first. Some advise to pay off the card with the highest balance first. Some advise to pay off the card with the highest monthly payment first. What to do!?

It is best to choose the method that makes the most sense for your individual situation. You may feel that it's best for you to have the least financial expenses in the long run no matter the current hassles, and decide to pay off the card with the highest interest first – even though it may be the card with the highest balance too, and therefore you won't be able to pay off the other cards with low balances for a long time. Or, you may feel that you would feel a lot saner if you only had one credit card to contend with, and so you may decide to pay off all the cards with the little balances first. The choice is yours and it all comes down to your personal priorities.

Begin by listing all your credit cards and debts. Next (in the right-hand column) number them in the order you plan to pay them off.

Creditor	Balance	Interest Rate	Monthly Payment	Card Payoff #
	$	%	$	#
	$	%	$	#
	$	%	$	#
	$	%	$	#
	$	%	$	#

At first continue to pay only the minimum payment due on all cards. Then follow the steps as shown on the next worksheet.

Step 1

Write down the card you assigned as your top priority to pay off.

If you can, during Step 1, try to pay extra – over and above the minimum payment required – to card number one.

Step 2

Once card number one is paid off, card number two becomes your top priority and you move onto Step 2, where you take the amount you were paying on card number one and add it to the amount you are paying on card number two.

Step 3

Once the first two cards are paid off, card number three becomes your top priority and you move onto Step 3, where you take the amount you were paying on card number one and two and add it to the amount you are paying on card number three.

Steps 4 through...

Continue on with the steps until you have finished paying off your credit card debt.

Step 1:   Date: _____

Credit Card #1 ....

Balance: $.................. Interest Rate: ....%

Monthly Payment: $ .... Extra Payment: $ .... Total Payment: $ ....

Step 2: (After Credit Card # 1 is paid off)   Date: ....

Credit Card #2 ....

Balance: $.................. Interest Rate: ....%

Monthly Payment: $ .... Payment for CC #1: $ .... Total Payment: $ ....

Step 3: (After Credit Card # 1 and #2 are paid off)   Date: ....

Credit Card #3 ....

Balance: $.................. Interest Rate: ....%

Monthly Payment: $ .... Payment for CC #1& #2: $ .... Total Payment: $ ....

Step 4: (After Credit Card # 1, #2 and #3 are paid off)   Date: ....

Credit Card #4 ....

Balance: $.................. Interest Rate: ....%

Monthly Payment: $ .... Payment for CC #1, #2 & #3: $ .... Total Payment: $ ....

Step 5: (After Credit Card # 1, #2, #3 & #4 are paid off)   Date: ....

Credit Card #4 ....

Balance: $.................. Interest Rate: ....%

Monthly Payment: $ .... Payment for CC #1, #2, #3 &#4: $ .... Total Payment: $ ....

Continue Steps as needed.

Final Step.   Date: ....

Celebrate (with cash)!!! You have paid off all of your credit card debt! WAY TO GO!

YOUR CHECKING ACCOUNT

It is also very important to know how much you have in your checking account at all times. These days some people don't keep their checkbook register updated and rely on an online balance. But your online balance is not an accurate portrayal of how much you have left in your account to spend, as it doesn't take into account checks that you have written, or payments pending, that have not yet been taken out of your account. Your online balance reflects how much your bank thinks you have left in your checking account, but your bank has not been told the whole story – that there are checks you have written that people or companies haven't turned in to your bank to collect on yet, or pending payments that haven't posted yet. Overdraft fees are getting to be quite high, and there's no point in having to pay these fees, which can spiral into a recurring problem. In your retirement it's very important to avoid easily preventable expenses, such as bounced check and overdraft charges, which can be $30 or more – each time. This is would be a large price to pay for a $4 special latte treat that you put on your debit card thinking you had the money in the bank – suddenly your little latte just cost you $34.

If you aren't balancing (sometimes called "reconciling") your checking account each month when your statement comes in the mail (or online – however you have it set up) only because you don't know how to do it, following are the steps you need to take. Also provided for you are a mock checkbook register and a mock bank statement. You can practice on these until you can balance your own check book.

If your checking account is beyond balancing, the best thing to do is to open a new account (without fees!), but be sure to leave enough money – plus a bit extra, just in case – in the old account to cover all the checks that you've written that haven't been cashed yet by the recipients. Once all the checks in your account have cleared, close that account. Be diligent from now on about balancing your checking account each month when your statement arrives (if you don't have your statement automatically sent to you either by mail or electronically, set up a monthly reminder on your calendar).

HOW TO BALANCE (RECONCILE) YOUR CHECKING ACCOUNT.

1. Check off the withdrawals (paper checks, automatic deductions, etc.) in your check register against the bank statement.

2. Check off the deposits (paper or automatic) in your check register against the bank statement.

3. Add up any outstanding withdrawals (those not checked off).

4. Add up any outstanding deposits (those not checked off).

5. Find and write down the ending balance from the bank statement. Add the outstanding deposit total and subtract the outstanding withdrawal total. These should equal the balance in your check register.

CHECKING ACCOUNT REGISTER MOCK-UP

This is what your checking account register should look like. The check marks that are already there are payments and deposits that were accounted for in the previous month's bank statement.

A	B	C	D	E	F	G	H
	CHECK BOOK REGISTER MOCK-UP						
				AMT. OF		AMT. OF	
	CHK NO.	DATE	TRANSACTION	WDL	✓	DEP	BALANCE
			Balance from previous page				2577.03
	4475	1-Jun	Exercise class fee	39.2	✓		
	4476	3-Jun	Books from Amazon	13.85			
		4-Jun	Reimbursed medical			20	
	4477	5-Jun	Latte and donut	10.65	✓		
	4478	6-Jun	Electrician - fix switch	144.1			
	4479	6-Jun	Domino's Pizza	21	✓		
	4480	7-Jun	Cash	100	✓		
	4481	9-Jun	Target	73.56	✓		
	4482	11-Jun	Counselor - co pay	20	✓		
	4483	11-Jun	Work lunch fund	30			2144.67
		13-Jun	VOID Chq. # 4476			13.85	2158.52
	AUTO	17-Jun	Water company	72.24	✓		
	4484	17-Jun	Dentist - co pay	34.32	✓		
	AUTO	17-Jun	Comcast - video acct.	66.17	✓		
			Balance from previous page				
	4485	17-Jun	Uninsured doctor bill	19.52			
	4486	17-Jun	Lowes - hardware	30.6	✓		
	4487	17-Jun	Visa payment	232	✓		1703.67
	ATM	19-Jun	Cash	40	✓		
	4488	20-Jun	Domino's Pizza	21	✓		1642.67
	4489	24-Jun	Work lunch fund	30			1612.67
	4490	29-Jun	Rent	1750			
	4491	29-Jun	Car and Life Insurance	167.16			
	4492	29-Jun	AOL	19.95			
	AUTO	29-Jun	Comcast - HSD acct.	46.21			
	4493	29-Jun	PSE - electricty and gas	185.27			
	AUTO	29-Jun	Brinks	35.99			
	4494	29-Jun	Verizon NW	95.24			
	4495	29-Jun	Verizon Wireless	121.26			
			Balance from previous page				
	4496	29-Jun	Charity donation	18			
	4497	29-Jun	Weeks Cash - 7/3	100			
	4498	29-Jun	Weeks Cash - 7/10	100			
	4499	29-Jun	Weeks Cash - 7/17	100			
	4500	29-Jun	Weeks Cash - 7/24	100			-1226.41
		29-Jun	Paycheck			3152.74	1926.33
	4501	30-Jun	Movie Theatre	25.5			1900.83
		3-Jul	Water heater			712.5	2613.33
	4502	5-Jul	DOL - car tabs	43.75			
	4503	7-Jul	Verizon - cell phone battery	43.55			
	4504	16-Jul	Loan to C.	120			2406.03
	AUTO	17-Jul	Water company	72.24			
	4505	17-Jul	Orthodontist	34.32			
	AUTO	17-Jul	Comcast - video acct.	66.17			
			Balance from previous page				
	4506	17-Jul	Photos	13.72			
	4507	17-Jun	Visa payment	232			1987.58
	4508	19-Jul	Domino's Pizza	21			1966.58
	4509	21-Jul	Target	34.67			
	4510	23-Jul	Office Depot - printer cartridge	18.32			
	4511	24-Jul	B-day check for cousin	20			
		26-Jul	Reimbursed overpayment			162.3	2055.89

BANK STATEMENT MOCK-UP

This is a mock-up of what a your bank statement looks like. Each bank lays out their statements differently and this one has actually been created on an Excel spreadsheet, but the information is the same.

Now look at the bank statement and the checkbook register and place a check next to each number that matches on both.

50

Once all the matches have been accounted for, you will have some left over figures in your checking account register. These are the "outstanding" payments and deposits that occurred after the last date of the bank statement. Now follow the steps above on a separate sheet of paper, or use the chart provided at the bottom of the mock-up bank statement. The number you end up with should be the same final balance that you have written in your checking account register.

BANK STATEMENT MOCK-UP   June 9, 20XX to July 8,20XX

CHECKING ACCOUNT

BEGINNING BALANCE	1816.29
DEPOSITS	3885.24
WITHDRAWALS	2949.92
ENDING BALANCE	2751.61

DEPOSITS

POSTED	AMOUNT	DESCRIPTION
8-Jun	20	Customer Deposit
29-Jun	3152.74	Best Company
3-Jul	712.5	Child Suppwashington-DSHS

WITHDRAWALS

CK NO	PAID	AMOUNT	CK NO	PAID	AMOUNT	CK NO	PAID	AMOUNT
			4491	3-Jul	167.16	4497	3-Jul	100
4478	9-Jun	144.1	4492	4-Jul	19.95	4498	10-Jul	100
4483	14-Jun	30	4493	2-Jul	185.27	4501	1-Jul	25.5
4485	18-Jun	19.52	4494	3-Jul	95.24	4503	8-Jul	43.55
4490	1-Jul	1750	4495	29-Jun	121.26			

WITHDRAWALS

POSTED	AMOUNT	DESCRIPTION
3-Jul	46.21	ComcastHSD
11-Jul	35.99	BrinksSecurity
12-Jul	66.17	ComcastVIDEO

RECONCILING YOUR CHECK BOOK:

ENDING BALANCE		2751.61
OUTSTANDING DEPOSITS	ADD	
OUTSTANDING CHECKS	MINUS	
CHECK BOOK BALANCE	EQUALS:	

HIDDEN HUNDRED

Here's a little trick to help you avoid overdraft charges, or to have a bit of cash available in case of (real!) emergencies. Keep a "Hidden Hundred" in your checking account.

Here's how: subtract $100 from your check register then use this new (fictitious) amount as your recorded balance. That way, you think you have $100 less than you actually do, so if you accidentally exceed your recorded balance, in actual fact, you haven't, and you won't get an overdraft charge. Just don't forget when you balance your checkbook each month to count that $100 as an outstanding check. The trick is, for this to work, you must forget it's there for the other days of the month!

FINANCIAL MUST-DO'S

Getting your finances in order is a consuming prospect, probably more than you thought it would be. However, the more you do now, the more solid a footing you will have in your Mindset Retirement. Following are some recommendations for you to consider for your retirement finances, but remember, ALWAYS adjust to your specific situation.

BANK ACCOUNTS

Go into your bank branch, and put P.O.D. (Payment on Death) instructions on all of your bank accounts. You should do this even if you are independently wealthy. It means that another person cannot have access to your accounts while you are alive, but if you die, the person you name can have direct and immediate access to your accounts, without waiting for what can be a lengthy legal process after your death. You can even put a minor's name, so if you want you can list any young children.

Keep a "hidden hundred" in your checkbook, in case of emergencies, overdrafts, etc. Subtract $100 from your check register then use this new amount as your balance. Don't forget when you balance your checking account each month to count that $100 as an outstanding check. Other than that, forget it's there!

The next time you order checks only have your first and middle initials and full last name printed on them, but always sign them with your full name. That way if someone steals your checkbook, they won't know what name to sign your checks with.

CREDIT CARDS

Write "Photo ID Required" on the signature strip of your credit cards. This means that every time you pay by credit card the clerk will ask to see your driver's license, but just smile and thank them for checking. It's a hassle, but the alternative of having your card lost or stolen and used, is even more of a hassle.

Make sure you have the toll free numbers of your credit card companies, which are printed on the back of your card, in a safe place at home (or store them in your cell phone) incase your wallet is stolen, so that you can call the credit companies immediately.

CREDIT

It's important to check your credit report annually. You can get one free credit report each year at www.annualcreditreport.com. You need to make sure that someone is not using your name or your credit. There are three main companies - Equifax, Experian and TransUnion - and each of them allows you to check your credit annually for free. This means that if you spread them out throughout the year, you can check your credit report once every 4 months. Put recurring reminders in your calendar.

A LINE OF CREDIT - ONE OPTION

They say you should have 3 to 6 months worth of income in savings. But for many of us saving 3 to 6 months of expenses is unobtainable at this time, even if you do have a job or own a house. However there is a way to have access to borrowing some funds in case of an emergency. If you have the option at this time, one thing to do would be to open a line of credit – both personal and business if possible - even if you don't need a line of credit at this time But do it now. Don't wait until you lose your house, lose your job, or otherwise have no assets, because just when you need a line of credit you won't be able to qualify for it. You don't have to make any payments now if you don't borrow from your line of credit, but this way you will always have a (fairly low interest) emergency "fund" to borrow from if you have not built up an emergency fund at far less interest than your credit cards. But, this all said, only use this option in the case of an extreme emergency and when you have exhausted all other options.

YOUR SOCIAL SECURITY NUMBER

Did you know that the first five numbers of your Social Security number tell when and where your card was issued. Which means that the last four numbers are unique to you only. For this reason, don't use them as a pin number, don't share them with anyone, and if possible try to use another number to identify yourself.

ONE SOCIAL SECURITY TIP FOR SOME DIVORCED WOMEN

And speaking of Social Security... We hear and read all the time that it's best to wait until you are 70 to claim on your social security, and I do believe that's true. And, anyway, you won't have to claim early if you are in a Mindset Retirement situation! But, there is one exception that I want to share with some divorced women.

Again, my usual disclaimer: I am not a financial professional, and I am only reporting what I believe to be the case at the time of the writing of this book, and my interpretation of it. And even if I am completely correct now, the rules may have changed by the time some of us are at an age to benefit. So, again, please consult with a financial expert or your Social Security office, but this is what I understand to be the case at this time:

If:
- ✓ you have been married at least 10 years,
- ✓ you have been divorced for at least 2 years,
- ✓ your lifetime income remains less than half your ex's,
- ✓ and – most importantly! – you don't remarry,

then:
you can qualify for half of the value of the social security benefits based on your ex's earnings, when you both reach 62 (although it's best to wait until the amount maxes out).

Even if your ex:
- ✓ remarries,
- ✓ hasn't retired
- ✓ hasn't begun to receive benefits himself.

Plus, your ex won't know when you start receiving your benefits.

And here's the really good news - the amount maxes out at age 66, not 70.

In my case, half of the value of my ex-husband's is more than the full value of mine will ever be, so the combination of being able to claim the maximum amount at age 66, and being able to claim more than my own Social Security amount, is a nice reward for a life time of single parenthood. (OK, well, of course my awesome adult children are my reward, but this is icing on the cake).

WHAT IFS

It is beyond the scope of this book to help you out in financial circumstances where extreme cases happen such that would render you completely unable to work. That doesn't mean that this book is only for the healthy, and that doesn't mean that one should not consider all the financial What Ifs – to not do so would be irresponsible. In an article in the November 2017 issue of Money magazine, Suze Orman reports that "About 30% of people...reported that they retired earlier than expected because of health issues." But whether you have no, or not enough, money for your retirement, and whether or not find yourself in a health crisis, you're still going to be better off with the right foundation and the right mindset. It also helps if the work you chose to do is something you could continue to do even if you were beset with an unexpected health issue (baring the extremes such as dementia and so on).

While I myself am thankfully pretty healthy (the usual age-related irksome ailments) unfortunately my own crystal ball is cracked, so I too want to be prepared financially for the worse. I'll share with you some of the things I have found out, although please remember that I am not a health expert, an insurance expert, nor a financial expert, and I am not in your shoes, so please consult with professionals whenever you need help.

HEALTH INSURANCE

One of the things that has helped me, being in the space between a full time job and social security is the Affordable Care Act. Regardless of your politics, it exists right now – at least at the writing of this book – and if it does change, I find it hard to believe that some sort of version of it won't still be available.

If you do need to find health insurance 'on the exchange' I highly advise finding yourself a Health Insurance Broker in your state. They will help you find the best insurance plan for your situation, and the best part is their services cost you nothing. They are paid a commission by the insurance companies, not by you. In my case, my insurance rate went from over $500 to $208 a month.

DIRECT PRIMARY CARE

Also consider Direct Primary Care (DPC) - also called *concierge* doctors or *boutique* doctors. You may have heard of this and thought it's not for you. True, it was once only for the rich and famous, but it's now an option for all of us.

How it works is that you pay a doctor a monthly fee directly – some doctors' offices term this as a "membership". This is regardless of whether you need the doctor that month or not. This may seem like a waste of money if you are healthy, but it's exactly what you are paying the insurance companies for. Wouldn't you rather it be going straight to your doctor?

You can enroll at any time and there should be no contract, which means you can withdraw at any time too. There are no co-pays beyond your monthly fee (unlike most insurance plans) and there are no "co-insurance" payments beyond your monthly fee (unlike most insurance plans). The DPC doctors that I've researched charge a monthly fee between $70 to $99. The DPC doctor I ended up choosing also includes in that fee:
- ✓ a comprehensive annual checkup, complete with an in office ECG (electrocardiogram) test and PFT (pulmonary function testing),
- ✓ an annual pap and Well Woman exam,
- ✓ a monthly osteopathic adjustment,
- ✓ a few miscellaneous services such as freezing warts, urinalysis, strep test, and so on.

Starting to sound pretty good? But wait, there's more.

The philosophy of these doctors, at least the ones I've met, is to do away with the 'middle man' (the insurance companies), so they have done the footwork for you to find additional ways to help you save money.

Some have partnered with a pharmacy and can get deeply discounted prescriptions.

Many have made deals so that you can obtain services - blood tests, mammograms, lab tests, imaging - at a nominal cost. For instance, an X-ray may cost you $60, or a blood panel may cost you between $9 to $36. But this is possibly less than your insurance co-pay!

You'll still need "catastrophic" health insurance for serious long term illnesses, injuries and diseases, but paying a doctor directly can be cheaper than paying an insurance company for all of these services. (I myself combine a DPC doctor with my ACA discount.)

HEALTH SHARES

Another option is a Health Share. These are usually run by religious or spiritual organizations, but in many cases you do not have to belong to the church, or even be "religious" to join. One such Health Share states only that you must agree that you want to keep your body healthy as "God" intended. There was no definition of what "God" should mean to you, and I think most of us can agree that we want to keep our bodies healthy.

Health Shares (which have to follow certain government guidelines) are meant to be instead of health insurance. And in fact if you belong to a Health Share you are considered "insured" by the government, and you are exempt from the penalties and fines set forth in the Affordable Care Act for not having insurance.

How Health Shares work is that people pay into a pool each month – I've seen between $150 to $250 a month for a single person (additional people, or a family, are discounted). This is the same concept as an insurance company, but without all the bureaucracy.

In some cases Health Shares will help with a discount on your monthly DPC fee. For instance, people signed up with a Health Share at my DPC doctor pay only $39 a month instead of $79 a month.

I'm not endorsing the Health Share concept, but I did hear a lot about them when I was looking for a doctor, and in fact, my own doctor uses a Health Share for his family. The main drawback I saw with the particular Health Share that I looked into was that you were not guaranteed payment in the case of an illness. Most seemed to have some sort of legalese clause stating that they were under no obligations to pay your medical bills. Plus, some online reviews, and reports to the Better Business Bureau that I read about some Health Shares had a common theme of non-payment of claims, or at best very slow payment of claims. Nor would some cover pre-existing conditions for a period of time; months or years. One would not cover injury or illness from "extreme sports", which included rock climbing. While some rock climbing can be extreme, if I was rock climbing in a gym with a belayer on a rope (which I do not consider an "extreme" sport), and I fell and broke my ankle, I would not be covered. Some stated that you could not use recreational drugs or drink alcohol excessively, which to me personally seemed reasonable, but may not to others.

I like to think that these bad reviews may have been unusual cases – how often do people take the time to write good reviews – but I just want to share with you what I found out. I can't really believe that these Health Shares don't have integrity - because if they did not, they would soon fold – but some of these restrictions were enough to give me pause. But, they are a viable option for you to keep your health costs down, and you should do your own research and make your own decisions.

GROUPON?

Did you know that Groupon is not just for saving money at restaurants and retail? You can also us Groupon for your health - doctor, dental and chiropractic, etc. Just be sure to check Yelp or other review sources before you schedule an appointment.

PET INSURANCE

What about our four legged family members? Our pets bring us such joy. Injury, illness or end of life are the hardest things we have to deal with. And we know that we will have to deal with these things at some time because our pets don't live as long as humans. After the end of life of my last cat – although she died naturally and thankfully her medical bills didn't cost a fortune – I decided that I never want to have to make a decision about my cat's health based on whether I can afford the treatment or not.

I've had pet insurance before, but it's been my experience that whatever my pet came down with wasn't covered by the pet insurance I'd been paying all along. If you have a pet, or pets, here's a suggestion for something I started doing when my cat came to live with us as a kitten. I decided to put $25 a month into an account designated specifically for any health issues my cat may have, and in particular end of life issues. He's now just over 4 years old and I had about $1200 saved up, plus interest! Just recently he came down with some urinary problems, and the vet visit and the lab test all came to $437! Ouch. But, I was able to "subsidize" myself – I could pay for some of it, but I was able to take $300 out of his "insurance account", which helped tremendously.

Again, this was my experience and my choice, and you may have had good experiences with pet insurance, so please do what you think is best for your situation, but please know that there are options out there with which you can empower yourself.

YOUR SUPPORT TEAM

If you've not been used to taking care of all these financial details before your retirement all of this information may feel a bit daunting. But, remember

1. you don't have to do it all at once, but it all has to be done, so just get started somewhere, and

2. you are not alone.

You probably already have a Support Team to help you out in your retirement - you just don't call it that yet. To empower yourself to know that you can retire, take a few minutes to create a list of your Support Team. Post it on the fridge or in your study, or keep it on your computer or phone. Here's a list of people to include, and you will probably think of more that are specific to your life and your situation:

- CPA (Certified Public Accountant, to help you with your taxes.)

- CFA (Certified Financial Planner) – once you have got on your feet.

- Attorney – if needed for personal issues, such as divorce, wills, etc.

- Attorney – if needed for business issues.

- Realtor.

- Medical professionals.

- Mental Health professionals.

- Handyman/plumber/electrician – I've had good experiences with reasonably priced contractors found on www.HomeAdvisor.com.

It's best if you can get a referral from a family member, friend or trusted co-worker, but if that's not possible, here's some tips about what I look for in a professional:

- (S)he or she has at least 10 years experience.

- (S)he advises you on what to do, but will also advise you *not* to do something. For instance, a lawyer who will tell you what the courts have ruled in the past and what your chances are now.

- (S)he is shrewd, but kind.

- (S)he has a good sense of humor.

- You feel (s)he genuinely cares about you.

- (S)he is prompt – turns up for meetings on time, responds to contact in a timely manner.

- Contact the appropriate organization that the professional belongs to check that (s)he has not had any complaints filed against them.

AARP

This isn't a plug for AARP (American Association of Retired Persons) per se, but I really think you should include them in your support team!

You don't have to wait until you are of "retirement age", you can join when you turn 50! In addition to receiving discounts on too many goods and services to mention here, you also get two magazines with a plethora of financial, health and lifestyle advice and inspiration for people age 50 and over. AARP also offers free workshops in their "Back To Work 50+" program, along with free coaching in some cases.

In addition, AARP advocates for, and are 'watchdogs' of, government policies benefitting people over 50. And for $16 a year (at the time of this writing) it's an expense of my Mindset Retirement that I feel pays for itself over and over again.

CHAPTER 6

FINANCIAL FIBS

"You are responsible for your own relevance."
- Unknown

Did you struggle to read through the last chapter? Or maybe you took one look at it and skipped straight to this one?

Why?

> Is it that you are bad at figuring finances?

> Are you no good with math?

> Not a "math person"?

Do you know you are fibbing to yourself!

WHAT IS A FINANCIAL FIB?

A Financial Fib is the story you've been telling yourself your whole life about money that you haven't realized is just a lie you've been telling yourself – and it has been affecting your finances all along.

Even if you are "good at math", if you are in the financial situation you are in now, chances are you've been telling yourself some sort of Financial Fibs.

Yes, many of us are in the Retirement Crisis because of outside forces, like the 2008 recession, divorce, a natural disaster, medical issues, job layoffs, and a variety of other forces beyond our control. However, we still have to take responsibility for how we handled these forces over the past years. Not everyone came through in the same way. What makes one person react one way and another person react another way? It's the stories we tell ourselves in our minds that we convince ourselves are "reality".

I came to realize that my financial self-talk was just fibs, and not reality, when I started to hear other people's fibs like the ones I listed at the start of this chapter. One person told me "*It is impossible to keep track of money*". Now I find this to be one of the easiest things to do (I didn't have much, but I was able to keep track of it). I heard another person say that they weren't very organized. Another person said they didn't have enough time. Another had a freezer crammed full of food she'd purchase in 2-for-1 deals, because she told herself she was saving money. There were as many fibs as people. It was then I realized, - because it *is* humanly possible to keep track of money, being organized and making time *is* humanly possible, and I don't find these things hard at all - that these were just these people's Financial Fibs. Which in turn made me realize that all of the things I thought, and said, and acted upon, and called reality about money, must just be Financial Fibs too. My own Financial Fibs had exacerbated, and in some cases created, my money problems.

Here's the main Financial Fibs I used to tell myself:

- People who are generous with their money are good people, and therefore I like to be generous.

- People who spend money on themselves first are jerks, and I don't want to be thought of as a jerk. As Suze Orman is famous for saying, "People first, then money, then things".

- I'm a 'socialist' at heart; I believe in sharing the wealth.

- There are always people worse off than me, so I should donate money on a regular basis.

GENEROSITY

All of these fibs had something in common - they fell into the category of Generosity for me. I grew up believing that I should be generous with money, but what I wasn't realizing was that I was always ending each of my Financial Fibs with

- even if it means putting it on the credit card.

I would spend money on things and experiences for other people (my kids, my family, my friends, my colleagues), but it would mean putting the expenses on my credit cards. But that was the only way I could keep my Financial Fibs as 'reality' in my mind.

ROLE MODELS

It was also my reality that one should aspire to be like one's role models. Who were my role models? My parents. My parents were middle class, and it really happened that they were generous with their money. But what I didn't stop to think about was that they were generous with their money

- only during the times when they had enough money in order to be generous.

Oops. I had made up a big story around what had actually happened and called it a "reality" that I had to live up to, even though I didn't have enough money to be so generous.

MORE FINANCIAL FIBS

But those weren't the only Financial Fibs I called "reality". Other Financial Fibs I had were:

- It's not worth saving any money towards my retirement, because a small amount won't make any difference.

When I was in my 20's my parents generously – *because they could at the time* – gave my brother and I about $8000 worth of stocks each. To this day I have no idea what happened to mine, but I know I somehow managed to whittle it all away pretty darn quickly. I do remember thinking at the time, that it really wasn't worth saving a mere $8000 towards my retirement, because that would only pay for a few months of expenses, and I didn't see how that would make any difference, so what was the point.

So I put away nothing towards my retirement, because my "reality" was that each amount was a futile amount so it's not worth trying to save anything.

- I'm bad at saving

I really was, at one time, bad at saving... chocolate. When we were young kids my brother and I would run down to the store every Saturday to spend our pocket money on chocolates. I would eat all of mine up, and he would take a few bites and put the rest in the fridge. And it would sit there. All week! From this childhood experience I concluded was that I was no good at saving anything - ever.

In order to keep this story as "reality" in my mind, a decision I made about myself as a young child stayed with me for decades.

- It's ok to buy it, it's only $20.

Or $10, or $25, or whatever. Twice a week? Three times a week? Each "small" purchase that I made surely wouldn't cut into my finances. The trouble was, in order to keep that Financial Fib as a "reality" in my mind, each time I made a small purchase I had to have my blinders on, and only look at that purchase, and consciously not remember anything else I might have bought that week. Suddenly my credit card was up in the thousands and I couldn't figure out why.

- It's ok to buy it if I've been wanting it for a long time.

If there was an item or experience I'd been wanting for a long time, and I noticed it again, or it suddenly became available, then I would immediately react and get it. I would justify to myself that because I'd been wanting it for so long, and had been so good waiting for it, that it was ok to get it – regardless of my current financial situation.

- Feast or famine. It's inevitable.

I knew that if the amount of money I have is low it will increase at some point. I also knew when my money increases somehow, it's going to decrease again at some point. It was the "reality" cycle of my life. So what was the point in saving. My Financial Fib was that it was good enough, sensible even, to create just enough money to get by.

- It will never be enough anyway.

When I did have money it still didn't seem enough. When I was married I was always on at my husband to earn more. Later during my single years, I was able to support our family on about a third of the income the household used to have. When I got divorced I felt like I'd dodged a bullet, because looking back I could see that I was falling into the 'executive wife - it's never enough' trap, and what would that mean about me?

I became afraid I'll never know when I have enough. So I created just under "enough". Since it's never "enough", it's not worth trying to save for, and I resented that I had to try.

- Money is stupid.

Money is a gauge of what type of person you are and how you treat others. If I actually like money, what would that mean about me? I would mean I'm a snob. But I'm not like those rich snobby people, so therefore money is stupid.

WHAT DO FINANCIAL FIBS MEAN?

In hindsight I've always managed to have a decent enough income in my life (either through a partnership agreement with a spouse or ex-spouse, or on my own). So I'd always wondered why was I always in debt and how was it I had no retirement savings. It was because I was living being true to my Financial Fibs without being aware that they were not "reality".

67

I also had to live in the 'money is stupid' Financial Fib, because in actual fact, I do like money, so in the context of my other stories, what does that say about me. So, in order to keep up the 'reality' of my Financial Fibs, I had to make money *mean* something. If I like money, I must *mean* I'm a jerk and it would *mean* that people will think I'm a snob. So it's just not worth it to create money because of what it *means* about me.

But, who said it means that about me?

I did.

So what do my Financial Fibs really mean?

Nothing.

Since realizing that my Financial Fibs didn't mean anything, I decided to let go of all that meaning. Which was hard, because that didn't leave me with any meaning.

And not having any meaning to live up to, I discovered that I was also using my Financial Fibs to cover up something else. I discovered that I was covering up having to take care of myself. And not taking care of myself – while appearing to do my best to take charge; you can't tell me what to do! – had a huge impact on my finances.

So I made a conscious decision to give up my disempowering Financial Fibs, and to start making empowering declarations.

ECONOMIC EMPOWERMENTS

I decided to declare my own meaning. Which in turn made me have to start looking toward other actions to empower myself economically. And suddenly ...I started acting on my declarations.

I stopped offering money I didn't have.

I started saving small amounts.

I started stabilizing.

I could see the big picture.

I was in control and I could spend and offer money thoughtfully.

Since this realization – and that's all it had to be, a realization – I have changed the way I handle money

You can too.

FINDING YOUR FINANCIAL FIBS

Look at what Financial Fibs you've been telling yourself are "reality". You've probably been validating your Financial Fibs you created when you were younger without thinking twice. Look back to your childhood, or your youthful years, and you will find your Financial Fibs. Look at how your own parents, and other childhood role models, talked about and handled money.

What were your Financial Fibs covering up?

Once you have recognized your Financial Fibs, ask yourself, what does money mean to you?

What does a *lot* of money mean to you?

If you like money, what does that mean about you?

If you had 100 times as much money as you do now, what would it mean about you?

Whatever you've made money mean - it doesn't mean that.

YOUR ECONOMIC EMPOWERMENTS

Your Financial Fibs are limiting you and defining you and leaving you with a way of seeing yourself that isn't reality. If you were to let go of your Financial Fibs, what could be your Economic Empowerments for your retirement?

But remember, revealing your Financial Fibs and creating new Economic Empowerments for yourself are only bandaids unless you take actions. So go back to Chapter 5 if you skipped over it!

Chapter 7

Mindset Retirement in Declaration

"Life isn't about finding yourself,
life is about creating yourself."
- George Bernard Shaw

If the Bog of Retirement chapter was the depressing chapter (how you got into this financial situation), this chapter is the inspiring chapter (ideas for how to transformation this situation).

In this chapter we will look at how to have the *mindset* of retirement without the *finances* of retirement. Because changing the "default" mindset you've fallen into and have just been living with will empower you to change your finances. And declaring your "new" mindset is the first step

DEFAULT MINDSET

Let's look first at how our "default" mindset can affect us.

THE *DIS-EASE* OF LACK OF RETIREMENT FUNDING

Whether your financial situation stems from a loss of employment, government financial crisis, natural disaster, health issues, divorce, or a myriad of other reasons, it's not uncommon to contract stress related diseases as a response. I know I'm not alone in experiencing physical symptoms in response to financial worries. Financial difficulty can take its toll on you, not only financially, but emotionally and even physically too.

In my case, when I went through my divorce (which is what my financial situation stems from) I had a heart attack, developed a brain tumor, got breast cancer and gained 17 pounds. OK, well, I didn't really, but I had all the symptoms. My chest hurt all the time and I developed costrochondritis (inflammation of the cartilage that connects a rib to the breastbone, which can mimic the symptoms of a heart attack), my skull actually changed shape and increased in size (my hats actually no longer fit, but a brain scan turned out to be, thankfully, negative), and I developed a rash that looked like inflammatory breast cancer (also, thankfully, negative). The 17 pounds weight gain was unfortunately real.

An article on anxiety in the December 5, 2011 issue of Time Magazine confirms that while some stress is actually productive "Excess stress hormones wear on the body...anxiety and stress have been linked to heart attacks, strokes, immune disorders, obesity, infertility and more...Collectively this creates a kind of chronic anxiety condition, with a nonstop series of stressors leaving us struggling with one crisis even as we're worrying about the ones to come."

The brain is not the only thing that reacts physically to emotional pain; the heart does too. In the book "The Heart Speaks" the author, cardiologist Mimi Guarneri M.D., studies people who'd had heart attacks, and compares their physical symptoms with what had been going on in their lives at the time, and found a very real connection to the physical and the emotional.

An article in the December 2011/January 2012 edition of Reader's Digest advises "Get help for depression. It doesn't just feel bad; it does bad things to your body".

Any *dis-ease* (as in: lack of 'ease') you may feel is very real. Consider the following symptoms. If you're in the situation where you do not have enough – or any - money for your retirement you, like me, have possibly experienced at least some, if not many, of these symptoms (in no particular order):

    irritability,
    poor concentration,
    exaggerated responses,
    depression,
    guilt,
    anxiety,
    panic,

pounding heart,
rapid breathing,
nausea,
muscle tension,
sweating,
avoidance tactics,
apathy,
difficulty falling or staying asleep,
nightmares,
aggression,
outbursts of anger,
jumpiness,
self blame,
shame,
hopelessness,
headaches,
stomach problems,
chest pain,
panic attacks,
phobias that seem random,
loss of interest in activities and life in general,
feeling detached or estranged from other people,
feeling emotionally numb,
sense of a limited future,
hyper vigilance; feeling and reacting as if you're constantly "on guard".

That's a long list of symptoms. This is actually a list of some of the common symptoms of Post Traumatic Distress Syndrome. Yes, not having enough – or any – money for your retirement can be that stressful.

YOUR PLACE ON THE PYRAMID

Before we move on let's do a quick review about the psychology of "needs", because if you are experiencing any of the above 'symptoms" I want you to know that you are not going crazy, and you are not a hypochondriac who is no longer interested in bettering yourself and your situation.

Remember the psychologist Abraham Maslow - he asserted that all humans have certain needs that are innate, and that some needs are felt more powerfully, and are more necessary to survival than others.

Those who don't have enough funds for retirement are usually stuck at one of the lower levels of Maslow's pyramid. As you will recall, Maslow called the bottom four levels "Deficiency Needs". In other words, these needs are taken for granted. A person doesn't really notice them as needs, unless they are deficient in them, at which point the deficiency becomes anxiety producing. It's when we go into a financially deficient retirement we didn't plan that this emotional and physical deficiency is accentuated.

Even though you may not have enough money for your retirement, you may still have wonderful friends, a close knit family, or are lucky to work in a supportive environment, have a supportive church group, etc., but the reality of it is that at the end of the day, financially you are still left clambering in the first and second levels.

It's at the fifth and sixth levels where we feel we fail the most if we haven't put enough away for retirement. This is the level where we start to compare ourselves to famous spiritual people and happy friends. Even Aristotle pointed out that if you are obliged to earn a living you cannot simultaneously be free. It's nearly impossible to focus on being completely committed to self-actualization when you feel you are struggling to make ends meet.

But do not put yourself on a guilt trip that you are not a 'good enough' person. Right now you are where you are on the Hierarchy of Needs probably because of a life-changing situation, not because you are a bad, unenlightened person. Your life will be more of a roller coaster for a while - recognizing and accepting that will make it easier to bear when you are not always at the top levels of the pyramid. Go on, say it to yourself – Wheeee.

NEW MINDSET

You are not going crazy and you are not an unenlightened person – you are going through a financial situation. "You" are not your financial situation. You may however feel at a loss as to how to handle this transitional phase in your life. That's why the rest of this chapter is full of tactics, insights, tips and ideas that I found helped me, that will give you the tools and motivation to climb your own pyramid as you progress through your retirement.

I know, I hear you, your financial situation wasn't entirely your fault – just at the wrong time your spouse left you for a younger model, your stocks plummeted, the natural disaster hit, you fell ill, your company laid you off, the whole economy tanked. I get that. But you can't change any of that now.

Perhaps your financial situation isn't entirely your 'fault' – the divorce, the economic crash, that act of nature, that jerk-faced boss who fired you – but admit it, it takes two to tango. Take responsibility for your contribution to your financial situation (see the Financial Fibs chapter!). Even if you find you cannot change the circumstances now, or if you truly like how the circumstances are now, if you do nothing more than recognize who you are and how you act and how it contributed to the dynamics of how you ended up in this situation, then you will at least have learned how to best find, and adjust, your modus operandi.

Recognizing and taking responsibility for your part of why you are where you are now, by getting to know yourself, means you are also taking responsibility for your retirement.

Remember how I said this was not a "How To" book? Well, it may sound like it is. However, all of the "how tos" I have assimilated into my own life and I offer them to you as choices. Not all of them may work for you as they did for me, but know that you have choices, and these are some of the declarations you can start using today to help you change your outlook as you enter your Mindset Retirement.

YOUR OUTLOOK

It's cliché, but it's true –

if you can't change the situation you can change your attitude.

I don't really like the term "attitude" I actually like to use the term "outlook". When I think of "attitude" I think of a sullen teenager giving lip, as if an "attitude" is something that is rude and unsociable. When I think of "outlook" I take the circumstantial blinders off my eyes, and I am Looking Out at the distance. I am Looking Out at possibility, I am Looking Out at choice.

Put the past where it belongs, behind you, and take care of your outlook for your future. Go ahead, imagine putting your past into a box, pick it up, hold it out in front of you (as you are used to doing), and then put it behind you, get up, and walk away into the new open space you've just created.

DON'T RUSH TO DO ANYTHING!

Lack of retirement funding affects each person differently, it affects people of different ages differently, it affects people in different situations differently, and it affects people who are in different stages of life differently.

Financial difficulty is also emotional, and however it affects you at the time is right for you. It may sound counter to some popular financial advice, but don't be in a rush to make any major moves or decisions. You need to work through any grief, anger, resentment and a whole host of emotional manifestations first. Also, out of chaos comes order, so you may soon be able to achieve things you didn't think you could before. There are events and people in the future that you don't know about yet. Allow time for those to come to your attention, before making any major choices or decisions.

In the meantime, taking the steps to feel comfortable enough to declare yourself retired may feel like a waiting game. I'm here to tell you that there's no rushing it! But I'm also here to tell you that one day you will look back and say, I'm glad that's all over, and be proud of yourself that you got through to the other side. When you start to go through the Mindset Retirement process, it's as if you are building a cocoon for yourself, where you have to retreat and regroup for a while in order to emerge as a beautiful butterfly. So go with the flow and know that as you go through the start of your Mindset Retirement, it's ok to be where you are, there's no rushing it.

EMOTIONAL CONNECTIONS

However, even if events won't be rushed there are things you can reflect upon and work on. One important facet of your life when you are retired is your emotional connections. For the longest time other people - people at your work place, or your kids if you've been a stay-at-home parent, or others - may have been your strongest emotional connection. But these are not the only emotional connections you had in your life. Deep emotional connections are good for the immune system and you can find emotional connections not only in other people, but also in, places, hobbies, and yes, even in some possessions (as you will read below)!

Emotional Connection with Friends

I can't stress enough the importance of staying connected with your friends, even if it seems such an effort to see them, even if it's inconvenient, because it's more inconvenient to be without friends. When I was starting the transition to my retirement my family was very supportive, but they lived in a different state, which made it a bit hard to just "hang out". So, I made a *huge* effort to e-mail and call my friends, schedule lunch dates, invite them to parties in my home and so on. I can't count the number of times before my retirement that a friend would say come and do this, or come and do that, and I'd think, I'm too tired, or I'm feeling too down right now or I have "too much to do", I'm going to decline. But now I make the effort to go anyway. If a friend wants to meet at a time that is inconvenient for me, I will re-schedule my other plans. Now some people may say that this is "accommodating". But to me this was "investing". And it paid off big time. This kind of investment has kept me rich in friendship ever since. The last thing I want to do is to lose my wonderful friends. Make time for emotional connections with your friends.

Emotional Connection with Objects

We often think of having an emotional connection with objects as being materialistic, or image conscious. But - it depends. True, some objects project an image, like the person who buys a red Corvette at the time of their retirement. The Corvette is an image enhancer. It seems to say to other people, I'm fast, I'm still young, I'm still fun, I'm rich and I'm better off now that I'm retired. Well, sure, it's debatable whether everyone agrees that this is the message a red sports car gives... but that's not the point of my story.

How a red Corvette can improve the quality of your life over an SUV or sedan, is beyond me. You still have to obey the speed limit, they both still get you from point A to point B, and they're both pleasant to drive. I see objects like a red Corvette as a materialistic, image conscious possession. However, if you buy an object because it enhances the quality of your life – for yourself (not for the purpose of enhancing your external image you show to others) - then that's an emotional connection.

For example, when I divorced, my ex got the 'good sofa'. I was stuck with this uncomfortable, rat infested (don't ask!) sofa bed. I put up with it for about a year, and one day something just clicked. I had some time to myself that day and I went to look at sofas. I found a sofa, a love seat and a comfy chair for $1100 – in brown (my favorite sofa color), in leather (my favorite sofa material), with a pillow-top (my favorite sofa style). I had no money. I bought it on credit (sorry Suze Orman). I sold the loveseat, because I didn't need it. I sold it for $300. So for $800 I had a leather sofa and matching comfy chair. To this day, 12 years later I love to sit in my living room on my sofa. Over the years I kept it as a "toy-less" room, and it was calming and nurturing. It's not something I show off to my friends, it's something I use myself. That sofa made a huge difference in the quality of my life, and still does, especially when I'm home alone on a weekend and I rent a movie. I love it!

The other "best move" I made after my divorce was to get rid of a patch of grass in front of my house and to hire someone to lay a patio. At the time I lived on a wooded acre of land. I really couldn't keep up with it all, and I didn't even try. But, that patch of grass in front of our house was where I spent a lot of my summer hours. It was under the drip line of a huge cedar tree and the grass was therefore tatty at best. I'd been wanting to install a patio for the better part of my marriage, but my ex didn't want to. Now my new patio wasn't something my neighbors could see, no one could see it from the street, it wasn't something that projected my image, and the earth soon settled so the paving slabs were all uneven, but my new patio made me very happy. In the summer I'd put an umbrella-table and chairs and the BBQ out there, and the kids and I used the area far more than we ever did when it was tatty grass – it was just so much more pleasant, and it improved the quality of our life. The patio was not just an object I bought; it was an object that provided us with a lifestyle that gave us pleasure. And even in the winter, every time I looked out my study window onto the patio, I'd find it very calming and it made me happy. At Christmas time I'd put up lights and it became a little "grotto" in the snow. I had a "Patio Party" at the end of the first summer that the patio was installed. This wasn't really to show off my patio, it was in order to have an excuse to have my friends over and to carry on a decade tradition of our family's annual summer party, with a new twist. After that my children and I would have a "Patio Party" at end of every summer. Sure, the first year my friends ooh'd and ahh'd, but soon it settled into a way to celebrate the quality of life I had with my friends. We focused on our relationships, not what we were standing on.

Those two objects, the sofa and the patio made me feel that I'm worth it – to myself. And now, at the writing of this book, now that all three of my children have finished high school and left home, I have downsized. I've moved from a 2400 square foot house on an acre of land to a 1200 square foot townhome in a pleasantly treed cul-de-sac. I joke that I have the World's Smallest Living Room, which may not be far from the truth. But again, the townhouse makes me happy. And – yes, my sofa and comfy chair just fit into my living room. And – yes, I removed the rotting deck and created a small, albeit gravel (for now), patio out the back door of my townhouse. I painted many of the rooms, got rid of the popcorn ceiling, and completely replaced all of the flooring before I moved in. Having pleasant surroundings has enhanced the quality of my life in my new home already, and I already have an emotional connection to it.

Now I don't advocate running around with your credit card and buying "stuff" to make you feel better when you retire, but I'm just saying, don't underestimate how the emotional connection to objects can better your life – if you're obtaining them for the right reasons, if you can afford them, if they're not purchases that will have fleeting use, and if they provide you with 'experience'. If you do have purchases you feel you need to make, ask yourself, will this improve the quality of my life, not, am I doing this in an attempt to improve my image to other people?

Emotional Connections with Hobbies, Activities and Sports

Hobbies can have emotional connections as well. The hobby I have an emotional connection to is ice-skating twice a week. I've been doing it for years. Don't get the wrong impression – I'm not any good. I don't like to go fast. I don't like to go backwards. I don't intend to ever let both of my feet leave the ice at the same time. Believe me, I am not doing this for the image. But to this day I have made ice-skating a priority - in my budget and in my time. I am doing it because it gives me exercise, it provides fun and friendship, and it is my 'meditation' when I concentrate only on what I am doing in the moment.

Emotional Connections with Family

Of course those of you Empty Nesters with (adult) kids have a built in emotional connection. I still *love* to have my kids visit me or visit them. Just spending time with them is a great source of emotional connection for me. So is spending my time hanging out with my parents and my brother whenever I get a chance to.

Emotional Connections with Someones and Somethings

Whatever or whoever it is, I found I need to foster emotional connections to all those someones and somethings in my retirement. If you don't have satisfying emotional connections in your life right now, think about how you can proactively go about changing that. One thing you can do is to look for a support group. Or, create a support group if you can't find one! Find like-minded people. I remember before I had kids that I looked down on mothers who would get together and talk diapers – how unintelligent. Once I had kids, I started a support group, and guess what we talked about? Diapers. It was fascinating...and most intellectual! If you're feeling alone and your working friends don't understand what you are going through and you're saying "why me", try saying "why not me" instead. There are a lot of people out there in early retirement, for whatever reason....so go find more "me"s to connect with. Heck – be in action – start a Mindset Retirement Club in your area! (As of this writing, there is no such thing, I've just declared it a reality – so go for it!) I've always believed, and experienced, that if you seek out like-minded people, together you will lead yourself to empowerment in whatever you chose to do in life, including throughout your retirement.

An emotional connection can literally improve your physical health. And by improving yourself, you are able to care for those around you better, a friend in need, an aging parent, adult children that need you, that stroppy neighbor you have to deal with, anyone. You always hear that you have to take care of yourself first. And sometimes we have a tough time with that. But think of it this way – when you are on an airplane, what do they tell you to do first in case of loss of oxygen? Right! Put your own oxygen mask on first before assisting others! So, budget in time for emotional connections for yourself. It will make going through your retirement just that much easier.

LIVING WITH YOURSELF

If you are single going into your retirement, you may be tempted to find a partner – someone to share expenses, share chores, share emotional connection – but while all our emotional connections are so important for our well being, don't rush into another relationship. Learn who <u>You</u> are first in your retirement. You may find that you are a different person now that you are retired and no longer on the treadmill. Different values, activities, and so on may become important to you. Only once you settle into this new retired life can you then offer that new <u>You</u> to a new relationship. Time and space will allow you to do that.

A friend of mine, looking back on her marriage relationship during her working years, admitted that now she could see that it wasn't the person she was attracted to; his values, his priorities, how he treated people in his world - it was the lifestyle that he had. In order to be a part of that lifestyle she had to accommodate. After retiring as a single woman she learned how to create her own lifestyle for herself, and now she pays attention to how people treat and interact with her (and others), before deciding if she cares to be included in their lives and if she cares to include them in her life. She now wants to hang out with a person who validates that she's a good person, worth knowing and spending time with, not someone who is always asking her to validate him where there is nothing to validate. She now turns away from many surface-level attractions that she would have been willing to accommodate in order to gain approval to in the past.

Once you've lived within your retirement for a while and have had a chance to re-discover your own values, you learn how to place limits on how you wish to be treated. Nonetheless, it is emotionally hard to be on your own, and let's face it, we all love the high of being in love and having a 'best friend' to hang out with. There's no reason that retired people can't find love – I had a friend who met someone in her 80's, and she told me it was as if they'd known each other their whole lives. But, it's unrealistic to think that everyone should have a best friend all the time. So find that natural high feeling with other emotional connections while

81

you settle into your new retired life. For me, it's being with my adult kids, going to lunch with my friends, watching a movie on my sofa, or sitting on my patio in the sun, and ice skating. I'm excited about these things – a warm thought to wake up to. Don't be in a rush to find someone new – find yourself first, then you'll have a best friend for a partner, who is truly attracted to who you really are.

SHOULD TO WANT

Let's face it, there's never enough time in the day – even when you're retired. It can have the power to drag you down, to make you think, 'I don't have time to do anything about my situation', 'I don't have time to plan to go to the moon, let alone actually build a rocket to get to the moon'. But, there is enough time, and it all boils down to priorities.

We'd all rather prioritize something we want to do over something we have to so. So, the next time you think about something that needs doing, and you say to your self "I *should* get it done", say instead "I *want* to get it done".

Change "should do" to "want to do" – because, let's face it, you actually do want that circumstance, or consequence of your actions to come about, rather than be faced with the consequences of it not coming about. For instance, when I lie in bed in the morning, I know I "should" get up. I like lying in my cozy bed, but it is also true that I do actually want to take care of some things today, and I do actually want to actively work on my Mindset Retirement plans today. So, instead of saying "I should get up", I say "I want to get up, because _____ *[fill in your own 'because']*".

Now sometimes you didn't want the things to do in the first place (such having to go through an early retirement with no money), but the alternative if you don't do them is not what you want either. So it truly is a choice that you are making when you say you *want* to deal with things that happen to you in your life. Even if these circumstances were imposed upon you, wouldn't you prefer to deal with them to your satisfaction than to have them go against you?

So as you go through your Mindset Retirement, every time you say to yourself that you "have to" or "should" do something, realize that you are actually "choosing" to do it. Even if it's the lesser of two evils, it's still what you would prefer to happen.

LIVING IN GRATITUDE

Notice things. If it was a pretty sunny day in the morning, but it clouded over by mid-day and chucked it down with rain the rest of the afternoon, say to yourself – it sure was nice to wake up to the sunshine this morning!

Life is not all bad. When I was going through my divorce I had to admit that I was grateful that I didn't have to move the kids out of their childhood home – so many people do. During a huge windstorm that hit my area in 2006 I had to admit that I was grateful that the trees that fell, fell on fences and a tree house, and that the ones that fell on my roof did minor damage, when so many other people had trees go through their second story to the ground floor. During the years when I had little money, I was grateful that I didn't live in a region devastated by poverty, wars, or extreme natural disasters.

While there's always someone worse off, this is not to say that if you break your arm and I break my finger, I shouldn't feel the pain. My 'broken finger' still hurts like heck, I still needed to heal it, and I still needed support, but I've found there's always some way to look at your cup as half full, not half empty.

In the Quotes section of the December 2011/January 2012 edition of Reader's Digest, poet Stanislaw Lec is quoted as saying "He who limps is still walking." When you are going through a retirement with scant finances, keep walking and live in proactive gratitude for all that you do have.

ALL THE EGGS

A Weight Watcher's leader once told our group a great story about being in the kitchen one day. She got a carton of eggs out of the fridge, but when she opened it up, she accidentally dropped one raw egg on the floor. It made an awful mess, with raw egg splattered everywhere. So, she thought, "oh well" and threw the rest on the floor, too! Of course she didn't really, but the point is that when one of your eggs breaks, don't throw the rest on the

83

floor – clean up the egg that fell and get on with making yummy omelets.

MIXING METAPHORS - PUT IT ON THE BACK BURNER, ETC.

I can't say "don't worry, be happy", because you *will* worry when your finances aren't what you'd like them to be. To a certain extent that's actually ok and can be productive, because it can spur you on to do things, like read this book, clean your bog, and start building your rocket on your sandy shores of your swimming hole. At the same time you do need to feel and deal with your pain, and you have a lot of details to deal with during this life transition. But rise above that as much as you can, and when on top of that allow yourself to focus on a layer of happiness. Remember that there are many other aspects to your life that haven't caused you pain.

There's no denying that an unexpectedly underfunded retirement can feel painful, and you can't necessarily stop your pain, but you can:

Practice Your Child Birth Breathing

Have you given birth to a child, or been present at a child's birth? Remember childbirth breathing? If you haven't had this experience, recall the image on TV of a panting woman, staring at a focus point on the wall. The concept is that if you focus on something else, the pain will lessen. Just like in childbirth you will always be aware of the pain of your financial situation, it's always there, but sometimes you have to breathe and concentrate on something else.

Hold It Out Kicking And Screaming

Or – think of it this way... Lesson the power of nagging doubts by holding the retirement out separately. It's still there, but visualize holding your retirement out at arms length, between your forefinger and thumb (try to touch it as little as possible!). Let it kick and scream as much as it wants, but right now you are busy curled up on the sofa with this book and a nice cup of tea, or you are busy having lunch with your friend, or you are busy writing out your plans to build your rocket, or you are busy recalling what a valuable person you were before this financial situation hit you. You don't have time for those nagging doubts!

Put It On The Back Burner

Or, in other words, sometimes you have to put your pain mentally on the back burner. This is not to say, put it on the back burner and forget about it. We all know what will happen if you do that – it will boil over. But remember to value the other aspects of your life, and realize you deserve them and put the pain of going through a retirement with no money on the back burner whenever you want.

INPUTS NOT OUTCOMES

Focus on the input of a situation, not the outcome.

The input is what you will do in a situation.

The outcome is what you wish will happen in, or because of, the situation. The outcome is a fantasy – it's you wanting to control what others will do or how they will react.

The only thing you can control is the input – what you will do.

For instance, if you need to look for a way to earn money during your retirement, the thing you can control is what your declarations are, and how you put them into action.

You can't control another person's decision or reaction – maybe the shirt you wore to an interview the reminded them of someone they don't like. Who knows.

Just know that you have the integrity to act your best and to empower yourself as you go through your Mindset Retirement.

DON'T LET IT GO, LET IT BE

I don't like to say "let it go", I like to say "let it be". Who am I kidding - it ain't goin' nowhere!

This isn't easy if something unplanned happened to you, such as a retirement with no money. But let if be what it wants to be, and get going with the rest of your life.

DISARMING NEGATIVE THOUGHTS AND SELF-DOUBTS

Negative thoughts and self-doubts are counter-productive. There are a lot of techniques for disarming the negative thoughts and self-doubts we all have when we don't feel financially secure, but these are a couple of my favorites about being "okay".

If this was "it", would I be okay?

When is enough enough? If, for the rest of my life, I had the friends I do, made the amount of money that I do, have the relationship with my children and family that I do, have the amount of 'me time' that I currently do, live in the place that I now live in, would I be okay? Even the richest person would like to be better off than they are now. I would go as far to say that almost anyone who lives in the western world (unless you are homeless and living on the street) is more okay than they think they are.

It's not to say your situation is brilliant – you may be living in "western poverty" – but I can't help but compare my situation to people in developing countries who live in tin shacks and have no toilets or potable water, or those who have had several loved ones die in warfare. The point I wish to make here is to practice gratitude for how much you do have and not focus on what you do not have, and you will see that you actually are going to be okay with what you have now.

At this moment in time, everything is okay.

It's hard to drive along in your car, or sit in your living room, or do the grocery shopping, without your mind running amuck about how "bad" your finances are, what you need to do, what you are finding it hard to do, how hard it is to go through a retirement with not enough money, and so on and so on. But make it a habit of stopping and asking yourself "at this very moment in time, is everything okay?"

At any given moment in time, is there anything you can actually do about your finances, while you are, for instance, getting food ready for dinner, or driving along in the car. *At that very moment,* is there actually anything wrong? If you were rich as all get out, *at this very moment* - what would be any different?

The key words are "*at this moment*". You'll be surprised at the amount of times you actually say "yes, everything is just fine *at this moment*". This isn't to say that you should stop being responsible for your life, but just to say that you should recognize that it's not bad all of the time. The more moments you can point out to yourself that things are actually okay, the more you will come to realize that there are actually more okay moments than there are bad moments, and that you are going to be okay.

CHOOSE SUFFICIENCY

Another way to disarm your negative thoughts, and help yourself through this is to change your self-talk about a lack of funds. If you are always saying to yourself I'm not buying this because *I can't afford it,* you are creating scarcity in your mind. Chances are, while you may be low income, you are probably actually doing ok compared with a lot of people in this world.

You probably do have enough money to purchase that latte, or that shirt, or that night on the town, at this moment. But ask yourself - do I choose to? Would you rather spend that money on something else? Instead of saying to yourself, or to others, "I can't afford it", say "It's not in the budget right now", or "It's not a financial priority right now". That says that yes, you do actually have the money to purchase that item, but you choose to have the money budgeted for something else. This mindset of choice gives you a sense of control and of sufficiency, not scarcity.

WHAT I LEARNED ABOUT MINDSET RETIREMENT FROM STAR TREK

There may be times when you may feel that someone is attacking you for working on a Mindset Retirement instead of a Financial Retirement. You may feel that this person, or group of people, feel that it is all your own fault for where you are financially at this point in your life, and that you should "be responsible" and get a well-paying full time job with benefits like they have. (Some people will say it's irresponsible of me to write this book!) And no amount of 'explanation' will appease them. You may be beginning to feel secure in your Mindset Retirement, realizing you will have "enough" and realizing that you will be ok, and that in fact you already are ok. But other people - whether they attack you outright or claim that they care about you and are acting in your best interests - can make you doubt yourself. Please realize that they are not the people with power and control over your life, you are.

When I was growing up I was a Treckie. I remember an episode of Star Trek where Captain Kirk, and (as per usual) most of the people important to the running of the spaceship, found themselves in an evil parallel universe - as one does. The way that evil Kirk had become captain in this parallel universe was to kill his predecessor. He now had to be on his guard all the time, because he had all the power and control, and the only way he would lose it was by his own death. Those who wanted the power and control were always trying to find ways to kill him. They acted aggressively, not because they had power, but because they didn't.

Don't forget this if you are "attacked" in any way, overtly, covertly, or with 'well meaning'. It may feel that another person is trying to exert a lot of power over you. But think about what they really want? What power and control do you have that they want? What is the motivation for the attack? Why are *they* feeling threatened that you are doing ok in your situation? What are *they* fearing about themselves? What are *they* afraid to consider about themselves? The mansion owner may be only one real estate bubble away from downsizing. The executive may be only one stock market crash away from an empty bank account. The CEO may be only one bad choice away from being asked to resign. Spouses may be only one affair away from poverty.

If you ignore them, they will try again. If they continue to try, it's because you actually have the power and control over your life, but for whatever reason they have to fight to keep power and control over their own *'never enough'* financial situation, and you're proving otherwise; you're proving you are doing ok. Suze Orman once said "when people are so vindictive and they're really trying to slam you, it's because they're so desperate – they're trying to do anything to get noticed. I just feel sorry for them". Always remember that in this sort of situation, if the other party resorts to attacks, it means that they have fears of loss of control over their own lives.

There is no reason for someone to attack you for your situation. There is every reason for your family, friends and acquaintances to support you in your situation. I hope you will never be attacked for the actions you are taking in your Mindset Retirement, but if you ever are, keep this in mind: it's because you have the personal power that they want. People can't manipulate you if you always act with integrity and maintain full responsibility and control of your life

DON'T TAKE IT PERSONALLY

Yes, you get it, but you still feel like you don't have enough money, at least not as much as your friends. And well-off friends can really grate on you sometimes with their lavish holidays, big houses, and new cars. You feel like you are the one being left out, why did this happen to you, you feel like you are the only one with no retirement funds.

It's a case of putting things in perspective. You can find yourself obsessing about what your friends are doing. But, think. There are a lot of rich people in this world. Do you obsess about all their lives and feel they're all grating on you? There are a lot of people with a lot of money in this world. Do you obsess about their lives and wish you were them? There are a lot of people who go on a lot of vacations. Do you really want to be on vacation all your life?

To help yourself along as you go through your Mindset Retirement, remember that your friends, family, and acquaintances are just a few of many, many people in this world, and you don't obsess about them, do you? And not only that, there are a lot of people richer than your friends, there are a lot of people who go on more vacations than your friends. Your friends are just a few of the masses.

Another reason not to fantasize about how great your friends' lives seems to be, is that you don't really know what's going on in their households, or in their bank accounts, and they're probably going to try to keep private anything negative that's happening to them. Give yourself credit for your own life, and don't take it personally if it appears that your friends are better off financially than you are now. You really are the one who is far better off with the fantastic retired life you are creating for yourself.

PRIORITIZING

Facing a retirement with little or no money can seem a bit daunting when it first hits you that this is what is going to happen – this wasn't in the plans! You may also feel a bit overwhelmed with all you have to do now. One thing you need to do is to decide what is a priority – for *you* – in your life. Everyone's will be different. Here's mine (I like to call them the 4 Fs):

1. Family

    Be there for them. If you have siblings, cousins, parents, adult children who don't live near you, it may be beyond your current budget to see them as often as you'd like. But in this day and age, thank goodness we have Facebook, and Skype, and e-mails, and texting, and the ability to take and send photos and videos with our cell phones (one expense it's hard to avoid, but look at all that little box in your hand can do!).

    If possible (and it's not always possible) be creative and search for, or create, retirement funding that allows you to be there for them as much as you can - without going broke of course. Later on you'll read about folks who sold their house, bought an RV, and traveled around the country funding their retirement. You have choices to make too. I myself use only an airline credit card. If I'm going to be having to purchase things anyway, I may as well earn free trips to see my family from time to time. If that is your priority, you can make it happen one way or another.

2. Funding

    You do have to fund your retirement, throughout your retirement, but remember, you are that person who, even if you were a multi-millionaire, would not be sitting around knitting and playing endless golf games once you were retired. Find what inspires you. Look at your own background for clues. If you don't know what you want to do, or what you can do, look back on the types of things you have been doing all along – how can you find a way to fund your Mindset Retirement that touches your passions?

3. Friends

Friends are very important, especially if you don't have family that is local and/or supportive. I can't stress enough how important it is to put an effort into spending time with your friends.

When he was 8 years old, I gave my youngest son his own e-mail screen name. He'd seen his sister who is 10 years older than him online all the time, reading and writing e-mails and IM'ing with several friends concurrently. Each time a new e-mail or IM would come in, her computer would go "ping". When he got his new screen name, my son couldn't figure out why the computer wasn't going ping and why he wasn't getting any e-mails. About twice a day, when I was online, he'd ask me to check if he had any e-mails. I told him "you have to e-mail people in order to get e-mails back". So we filled up his address book with names (people whom I knew would be safe and responsive) and he started writing e-mails, and lo and behold, he started getting e-mails back! It's most important when you are going through your retirement to reach out to your friends – don't expect them to reach out to you no matter how much they may enjoy your company. They may just be too busy to think to take a break themselves, or they may think they are doing you a favor by giving you time to yourself. Sometimes it's up to you to set up that lunch date or walk date, host that potluck party, and send those e-mails!

4. Fitness

We all need time to ourselves to exercise. You won't feel fit to fund your retirement if you aren't fit in general. When entered my retirement I had little money and little time for my health. So one thing I did do was to walk around the neighborhood each morning. It always took 17 minutes and I walked at a fast pace (a "stroll" never lost anyone any weight!). It wasn't much, but at least I was doing something. Many people feel that they can't take the time to exercise, but remember the analogy – when you are in an airplane, the flight attendant tells you to put your own oxygen mask on first, then help others. If you're not functioning well you can't have the stamina to be there for everything you need to do. More and more we see stories in the media about how taking a break actually makes you more productive in the long run.

Whatever your top priorities are, think about what you need in order to get through your retirement. Prioritizing can give your life focus, sort of like a Mission Statement gives a company focus. My life and my choices in life revolve around my priorities – for instance almost every choice I make revolves around my top priority; being available to my family. It affects the job I choose, the importance of keeping myself in good health, and the types of friends I choose. What are your priorities and how will you adjust your life to support them?

QUIT!

Of course you can't do it ALL when you are going through your Mindset Retirement. Prioritizing those things you can do, means that some things have to go by the way side that might not have under other circumstances. Some things you just have to get done, but some things really could just be nixed.

Knowing what to quit and when, is half the battle. For example, if you've always headed up a committee at your church or volunteered at a local school, just because you've put a lot of effort into it in the past and it's become your "baby" and others have relied upon you for so long, is not a reason to keep up with that activity now. If your decision to keep a commitment that is now a hardship to you is based on the past – quit!

Make a list of everything that is in your life. For me, I've never had a great love for gardening, baking, clothes shopping and the such. Things that take up your physical time, things that take up your mental time, things that cost you money, things that you think you have to do, things that you think you ought to want to do, things that must be done now, things that could be put on the back burner or 'pruned' off your tree of life. When you write things down you will probably be amazed at how long your list is.

Now here's the catch, you have to be ruthless when it comes to putting your prioritized needs first. For instance, a lot of people give a lot of volunteer hours on other people's behalf – directly or indirectly. This is awesome – if you have the time and money to do so. This may be news to you, but your charity-of-choice will survive without your help.

I used to have a "Sticky" on my computer's desktop that read:

Does it support....
my family,
my retirement plans,
my home,
my health,
my friendships?
If not, don't waste your time on it!

I saw it when I logged in every day. Sometimes you have to remind yourself not to take on too much, and that you don't have to do everything perfectly.

I'm not saying this pruning will continue on forever. It's just that someone else will have to save the world right now. When you're more stable in your retirement then maybe you can be that person – if you still want to... Remember Maslow's Hierarchy of Needs. You have to support your own basic needs first or you have no foundation on which to support anything else.

FIND YOUR "NESS"

For those of you who aren't currently in a relationship and can't help thinking how that would fix all of your financial retirement woes - please don't jump back into a relationship. As I mentioned previously, give yourself time to find out who you are without another person in your life.

In the movie "You, Me and Durpree" Owen Wilson's character Randolph says "You've got to find your "ness"." For example, I have to find my Beth-ness. No one but me has *my* Beth-ness. There are other Beths out there, but they have their own Beth-ness. Rediscover who you are. Don't rush into anything. And allow your Mindset Retirement time to settle down before you make any major moves.

LEAVE PEOPLE BETTER THAN YOU FOUND THEM

Even though you may feel like you are the one going through the tough time, it helps if people around you are pleasant too. Sometimes they're not. But, if you've ever been in Scouts, you'll remember that we always leave the campsite better than we found it . The same can go for people too. Just a small action or quick word can cheer someone up, and if the people around you are cheered up, you can be too. I always like to leave people better than I found them. It's fun!

PUT THINGS IN PERSPECTIVE – TEN YEARS AGO

Your Mindset Retirement won't be a bed of rose every minute of every day – nothing ever is. There are going to be irritating things that are going to happen. But, it doesn't mean you have to buy into becoming irritated.

I want you to think about something irritating that happened to you about ten years ago. Think about how you felt about it at the time it was happening. Rate that on the irritation scale from 1 – 10. Think about how you feel about it now in the scheme of things. Rate that on the irritation scale from 1 – 10. It probably doesn't bring up the same feelings or irritation that it did at the time ten years ago.

So, the trick here is that for every irritating thing that comes along, that you think about, or that the Committee In Your Head talks to yourself about, add the words "...about ten years ago..." to your sentence and see how much you *really* give a hoot!

Now this is not to say that the thing (or person) that is irritating you should necessarily be let off the hook, but we can't keep on about everything irritating thing that happens to us, or we'd go crazy. While I don't like the phrase "don't sweat the small stuff" because the small stuff sometimes piles up, you can put things into perspective by adding the words "about 10 years ago" to help lesson the frustrations that will come up in your Mindset Retirement.

JUST GET STARTED

As I've mentioned before, it's great to declare you are going to the moon, but you then have to be in action about cleaning up your bog and building your rocket on your sandy shores. You don't have to know all the answers to "how to be happy in a retirement with not "enough" money", but you do have to be in action. Sometimes you may not know what to do to be in action.

A wonderful high school math teacher told me, when you are faced with a complicated math problem - just start doing something. Write down what you know. Re-write the problem in your own handwriting on the paper. Manipulate it anyway you know how. By just starting, it will bring other ideas to you.

Now, unlike a math problem, the perfect solution may not always come along when you are planning your Mindset Retirement, but life allows for making choices and letting go of choices. You don't have to know the outcome yet, so Just Get Started doing *some* action, and the choices will start to become apparent. You may have to course correct at times, but don't let that stop you. Just get started on your journey.

Chapter 8

Mindset Retirement in Action

"A ship in harbor is safe -
but that is not what ships are built for."
- John A. Shedd

Now that you're in the Mindset of your new retirement you're ready to put your declarations into action. The best way to do that is to keep everything in order and organized. It makes it a lot easier.

My friends always tell me they think I'm so very organized, but I tell them, I'm not really. I'm only organized because I'm lazy and I'm a flake. The actions of organization make things easier and quicker in the long run, and I really want to do as little work as possible. Plus, I have a terrible memory – if I wasn't organized my memory would get the better of me and bring out the worst in me!

Since my divorce (which was the 'force' that threw me into my Mindset Retirement – yours may differ) I have come to acknowledge that for the longest time I did everything "half assed". I had to do twice as much as I once did. I had to be mother and father (in fact, I was the one who taught my two sons how to shave!). I had to be wage earner and housekeeper. There was no way I could do everything as well as I used to.

Remember Nancy Pelosi. We're not all Nancy Pelosis, nor do we have the financial backing she had from her husband, but if she can enter the work world at age 47 and create a retired life up to age 77 and presumably beyond, so can we!

Did she do it all? Yes. Did she do it all at the same time? No. Nor can you. In fact, Lesley Jane Seymour, editor of More

Magazine debunks the myth that you can do it all. "Work-Life Balance is a Crock" she writes in the December 2011 issue.

There's only a limited amount of time in a day and a limited amount of energy in my mind and body, so twice as much only gets half done. You can still have a good work ethic, but you have to learn to know when something is good enough. Or if you want to give something 100%, then you give that one thing 100% at that time, and at another time you can give another thing 100%. Only you will know what is the best choices to make in your situation.

This section of the book looks toward your new retirement and how you can find the resources and inspiration to help you move into your Mindset Retirement. You can have it all - just one step at a time.

1. PRIORITIZE. 2. PRIORITIZE. 3. PRIORITIZE.

When you first enter your Mindset Retirement your Action To Do List can be overwhelming. It's important to prioritize your chores, errands, paperwork, repair list, needs and wants, and so on and so on and so on and so on....

There are many techniques for prioritizing your Action To Do List; here are some suggestions.

THE COMPARISON TECHNIQUE

Here's how it works: Let's say you have a list of ideas of how to make or save money. Take the first two items on your list, compare 1 with 2. Ask which will make or save me more money. Say it's #1. Then compare #1 to #3, and ask the same question. Keep going. Perhaps #1 wins out until you get to #7, then when you compare #1 with #7 you find that #7 is the better choice. Continue on now comparing #7 to #8, and so on. Always using the "winner" until you get to the bottom of your list. That will be your first priority. Now start doing the same thing with #2. Do this until you have three to five priority actions that you can focus on first. It doesn't mean that if #6 lost out all the time, but suddenly an opportunity came along to fulfill #6 that you shouldn't take that opportunity, but in general, focus your time and efforts on those major activities that will either make or save you money the quickest or the most. Then focus on the things that will directly and quickly bring in (or keep on bringing in) money into your life, or stop it leaving your life.

THE EVALUATE AND FOCUS TECHNIQUE.

This is another way to prioritize about making or saving money. Evaluate the items on your to do list in terms of what will most make or save you money. Then focus on the things that will directly and quickly bring in (or keep on bringing in) money into your life. For instance, give up giving time to your volunteer positions, at least for now – they'll always be pleased to have you back later on and can do without you for now. And/or give up (at least for now) any *speculative* plans you have (for instance starting a new company or writing a book), *unless* you are very positive about their outcome. Stop seeing people who zap your time, money and focus. At least for now, focus only on the "sure bets". Let other time and money zappers go.

THE REMEMBERING TECHNIQUE

Here's a technique for remembering to get things done. Let's say you have to remember to do two things. Do the thing you that you will most easily be reminded of last. For example, you are leaving the house and you want to remember to take off your slippers and to pick up your car keys. Take off your slippers and put your shoes on first. You won't have to be reminded to pick up your car keys, because you can't go far without your car keys, but you can go miles in your slippers.

THE URGENCY TECHNIQUE

This is a similar technique to the remembering technique. Do the thing that's more urgent first. If it is not urgent and you forget it, chances are you'll remember it down the road. For instance, before you go to bed, you want to remember to call someone about an important issue in the morning and run the dishwasher. Write a "note-to-self" about the phone call first. If you forget to run the dishwasher, it may be inconvenient but it's not the end of the world.

THE FOUR QUADRANTS TECHNIQUE

Here's a good technique for those times when you have a mile-long to do list .

Divide a piece of paper into 4 sections or "quadrants". Label the two sections across the top Must Do and Want To Do. Label the two sections down the side Urgent and Not Urgent. Then re-write your to do list, putting each item in one of the four sections. Go through your to do list in this order of quadrants.

1. Must Do Urgently
2. Must Do but Not Urgent
3. Want To Do Urgently
4. Want To Do Not Urgent

Of course, as soon as you cross one thing off, you think of another (or another thinks of you) for the Must Do or Urgent quadrants and it feels like you will never get to your Want To Do items, so once in a while make sure you do an item or two from the Want To quadrants in order to keep your sanity!

THE JUST DO IT TECHNIQUE.

Sometimes you just can't prioritize, it's all important. If it is the case where everything has to get done within a time frame, then it doesn't really matter what you pick first as it all has to be dealt with eventually. As long are you are dealing with one thing, you are making progress.

MAKING CHOICES AND DECISIONS

Sometimes you haven't even got to completing your Action To-Do List because choices and decisions have to be made first. This too can be overwhelming, but there are some techniques for making choices and decisions too. Here are a few.

THE WAITING IT OUT TECHNIQUE

If you find you can't make a decision about something, it may be because all of the factors haven't come to light yet. If at all possible – wait. Eventually just one piece of additional information may make it clear what is the best decision.

THE TRY IT OUT TECHNIQUE

Alternately, if it doesn't really matter right now which decision you make, just try one out. If it doesn't feel right, try the other. You'll soon know your answer. When I'm directing a play and the actor says I don't know whether to say the line this way or that, I say "Try it both ways.". It immediately becomes abundantly clear which reading works. If you can't sort something out mentally, try it in reality.

THE INTUITION TECHNIQUE

Sure, we're all meant to have intuition right? Well, my intuition says I will buy a ticket and win the lottery tomorrow. Suddenly that makes me all tense with something that is a cross between anxiety and excitement. Or do I feel that way because I really, really desire to win the lottery tomorrow? How do you know if something is intuition or desire? It's been my experience in life that intuition has no emotion. You are drawn to something, and you know no reason for it, nor do you feel any emotion about it, positive or negative. You just know that you are going to do it - or not do it.

THE DECIDING AND MOVING TECHNIQUE

You can't always peer into your crystal ball when it's all foggy, and see how your decisions are going to turn out. But, in order to be in action, it's important to make some sort of decision. If the outcome of the 'right' choice is not clear, decide on something and move in that direction. Pretty soon, because of your movement, it will become clear if that was the right decision for you. If it was, keep moving. If it wasn't, decide again and start moving in another direction. Repeat. Pretty soon, in your next movement, it will become clear if that was the right decision for you. If it was, keep moving. If it wasn't, decide again and start moving in another direction. Repeat. You get the idea. Keep deciding and moving, deciding and moving, deciding and moving, until such time that you find yourself just moving.

<u>THE DETACHMENT TECHNIQUE</u>

How can you detach from an outcome? Know that the only thing you have any control over is how much and what input you create. You never have any control over the outcome – never! The perfect solution may not come along, but life allows for many choices along the road, which means sometimes you just have to let go of some outcomes. You can't possibly fit them all in anyway. So do your best and detach from the outcome - it is beyond your control.

BEING EFFICIENTLY ORGANIZED

You may feel that right now you have been forcedly thrown in to a Type A personality lifestyle. No matter your real personality, you may be feeling at this time that you are working non-stop to catch up. You may be dreading a retirement of drudgery, especially if you are not a particularly organized person.

So, in order to be able to deal with your new retirement plan you do need to learn to be efficiently organized. But, "efficiently" organized doesn't mean "perfectly" organized. If something is efficient it means it "works". Don't try to strive for perfection, it's simply not possible.

Following are some (free or cheap) tips on how to be organized in your retirement. It seems like a long list, but you don't have to do it all right away, or at all. Look to the future, some you can do now, some later, some not at all if they don't suit you or pertain to your situation. Here goes...

<u>RECORDS AND PAPERWORK</u>

- Buy a fire-proof box (about $30-40 at an office supply store) for all your legal documents. If you can afford it and have space, buy fire-proof filing cabinets. They store more than a box and can't easily be stolen or broken into, as well as being safe from a fire.

- Photocopy the contents of your wallet (both sides of cards) and your passport. Keep a copy in your fire-proof box, and send a copy to a trusted relative or friend to hang onto for you. When you travel abroad (never say never!) have each member of your party carry a photocopy of one other person's passport.

- Document all your possessions by photographing them and listing them on the back of the photo. Keep copies in your fire-proof box, and send copies to a trusted friend or relative. Possessions such as: jewelry (even 'cosmetic' jewelry), electronic equipment, plates and dishes, furniture – basically anything that's not bolted down, and some things that are.

- Know what's on your Medical Report. Contact MIB (Medical Information Bureau) – it's like a credit-reporting agency for healthcare. Your file only contains information that you've given to insurers, not your actual medical records, but it could influence the cost of your premium and whether you can obtain individual health, life or disability insurance. Check it periodically to make sure the information is up to date and correct. For a free copy of your MIB file, call 866-692-6901.

- Keep track of your expenses – food, shelter, health, etc. Do this for 3 months and then find the average. That way, you have a record of the real cost of your retirement and you will know what you are aiming for – or where you can cut things out.

- Update (or create) your will, trusts, health care directive and/or Power of Attorney.

- Update your life insurance beneficiaries.

- Update your retirement plan beneficiaries, if you have any retirement funds, no matter how small.

- Put P.O.D. (Payment on Death) on all bank accounts. It means that another person cannot have access to your accounts while you are alive, but if you die, that person can have direct and immediate access to your accounts.

- Wondering how long your appliances will last? According to www.thisoldhouse.com, these times are quoted by The Association of Home Appliance Manufacturers:

Air conditioner	10 yrs.
Dishwasher	10
Dryer	14
Electric range	17
Garbage disposer	10
Gas range	19
Microwave	11
Refrigerator	14 – 17
Washing machine	13

BIRTHDAY LIST

Happy Birthday! This checklist is your birthday present to yourself. Some of these may cost some money, but, hey, it's your birthday, you deserve these 'gifts'! Take care of these annual chores and errands during your birthday month each year and you'll never forget to do them.

o Schedule your annual doctor's check up.

o Schedule your annual imaging and screenings.

o Schedule your semi-annual teeth cleaning.

o Review your life insurance policies if you have them. Make an appointment to make any changes (or get rid of it if you no longer have dependents).

o Review your homeowner's or renters insurance. Make an appointment to make any changes.

o Review your will, trust, health care directive, power of attorney. Make an appointment to make changes if anything has changed within the past year.

o   Check your car manual for routine maintenance needed. Check your car for the need to rotate, balance, align tires, change the oil, fill wiper fluid...

o   Get your FREE annual credit report at www.annualcreditreport.com.

o   Every three years, if you have a fireplace, have your chimney cleaned.

o   Clean your air conditioning/heating ducts once every couple of years.

o   If you have a septic tank, instead of a sewer system, have that pumped about every two or three years.

o   Check your cell phone contract. Is it about to expire? If so, can you get a better deal?

Chapter 9

Funding Your Mindset Retirement

*"I really need nothing more than this log-cabin
offers. But elsewhere one must have a house and
servants, and burdens and worries...the "thick clay"
in the shape of "things" which one has accumulated."*
From:
A lady's life in the Rocky Mountains
By Isabella Lucy Bird

I can't tell you how to fund your Mindset Retirement, but I can
share what my choices were. Association – one idea triggering
another (the technique of brainstorming) - is a good way to
inspiring you to discover your own Mindset Retirement funding.

As I've mentioned before, throughout my marriage, with raising
my children as my top priority, I continued to work in my field on
and off whenever I could. Sometimes for free, sometimes for a
nominal stipend. My ex called it "dabbling". However, in the
professional world this is called "keeping abreast of your
profession". Without this "dabbling" I doubt I would have been
prepared for being thrown into a Mindset Retirement instead of
the Financial Retirement I had expected.

But I don't feel it's worth my time and mental energy speculating
about what my alternate retirement might have been like. I, like
you, have no choice, and so the best thing we can do is look
towards our New Retirement.

You too have some sort of history that you can look back on. If
you were like me, maybe you worked part time, perhaps you did a
lot of volunteer work, perhaps you didn't work at all during your
marriage, maybe you'd planned to go back to work once your kids
were older. Or, perhaps you had a full time job in the work world

for some decades, but lost it for a variety of reasons. Perhaps you are still working now, but you lost all of your savings in 'the crash'. Regardless of how you got here, now you are struggling to find the funding to make ends meet. But you can do it.

In my case I used my teaching skills, design skills, management skills, and writing skills, all of which I'd done at different parts of my life, and consolidated all those crumbs into the bread-winning Mindset Retirement that I have now. Remember Hansel and Gretel? Look for and follow your breadcrumbs.

Obviously you can't choose from just any situation, or even from my list, you have to have some aptitude towards the work you are looking to do. So, consider, what are you even the slightest bit interested in that might bring in the bacon? If you can find something, anything, that "interests" you, you can choose to put your attention on that and start to develop that area. That which you give your attention to will grow.

ONLINE

Before we look at some specific ideas, please know that this is actually a very good time to be in a Mindset Retirement. Because of.... The Internet! You can easily search for inspiration. You can easily search for work. You can easily sell your own wares. You can easily provide services. You can easily teach online. You can easily create your own website. You can easily publish a book.

By "easily" I mean it's all there provided for you, at your fingertips. That's the Declaration part. You get to follow that up with the Action part.

Here's some ideas that might trigger associations for you, that will in turn give you some ideas for how to fund your own Mindset Retirement.

JUST GET STARTED

THE DUMMY JOB

The first way of funding your retirement that you find just in order to put food on the table might not be your main passion.

Sometimes you have to give up something to get something else. Sometimes you can't always follow your biggest passion because it not practical at this time. But this isn't to say you have to completely give up your big passion, you may simply just have to put it on the back burner for now.

As long as you experience some success at this stage, while it may not be your ideal, you are contributing to your Mindset Retirement. Later on down the road you can apply the new skills and knowledge you've learned to something more suited to you.

CREATE

DESIGN

Do you have website design, or other, technical design skills? I know of someone who spends his time traveling around the world doing charitable work. He didn't earn his millions and retire early. He is in a Mindset Retirement. But the way he funds his Mindset Retirement is as a website designer. Website design is done primarily online so this enables him to take his website design work wherever he travels.

CRAFT

Are you creative in a hands-on way?

Have your friends always told you your house is beautiful, or your garden is so pleasant, your photographs are amazing? Do your friends always tell you how beautiful your furniture pieces are? Do you paint or draw? Can you create physical objects to sell?

If so, you are in a good day and age! You no longer need to rely on word of mouth, or sit at craft fairs (although those are still valid too). There are many online "stores" where you can sell your wares. Or you can create your own website, Facebook page, LinkedIn account, and so on.

CARETAKE

HEAL

I've never been much of a physical healer, but a friend of mine recently opened her own massage therapy service. Do you have past healing, medical, spiritual, psychology skills that you can apply today?

LOVE PETS

Live in a city or suburb? Think: dog walking services, pet sitting services.

ORGANIZE

Is Organization your middle name? Can you organize closets, filing cabinets, kitchens, lives? There are a lot of people out there who are willing to pay you to do so.

TEACH

What skills – mental or physical – do you have that you can teach to others?

TUTOR

Are you good at math? Can you play a musical instrument? Are you a photographer? Do you speak another language? You could at first work for a tutoring company, even though they pay low hourly rates, but then once you've learned the ropes, you could become a private tutor. A private tutor can earn a decent hourly wage. Also, if you're tutoring in a subject you're passionate about, it's very rewarding too. Be sure to create your own website, too!

EXERCISE

Do you have a physical skill like dance, yoga or jump rope? Particularly skills that don't require much equipment to do?

Consider offering a course at a local community center, a local hall, or even in your home if you have the right space.

SUB

Did you know that in some states you don't have to have a teaching certificate to substitute teach? Some states only require that you have a Bachelor's degree. That does mean that the person with a degree in Underwater Basket Weaving can sub in a calculus class – maybe not the best situation for the students that day – but it does give you some opportunities. Most states are usually hurting for substitute teachers, so if you like working with children, this can be a great source of funding and fulfillment.

COLLEGE INSTRUCTOR

You don't have to be a professor to teach at a college. Many colleges have online course and/or community courses. I once taught an evening course on residential and landscape lighting. If you have a skill and a knowledge to share, submit a course proposal at your local college. You'll not only get paid, but you never know what that will lead to.

CREATE YOUR OWN ONLINE COURSE

Do you have enough knowledge and skills built up to create a whole course? Consider creating a whole online course. That's what I did. And it doesn't have to cost you a lot to set up. I've taken online courses before, and I wanted to use the same format that I've used in universities, but I looked into purchasing such a program and it was prohibitive. But with the tools available online today I was able to create the same format of engagement for my students, without the brand name template. I now teach a 10-week online course in my profession once a quarter. It's one of my funding sources for my Mindset Retirement. And, because helping others to achieve success in my field is something I'm very passionate about, I get a lot out of it too.

SHARE

You've probably heard the term the "Sharing Economy". Now is your time to cash in on it. Do you have stuff or property to share? Apparently Americans over 60 are the largest growing group of room and property rental hosts, so why not jump on the sharing bandwagon. Check out these websites (I do not endorse any of these sites, plus there are many more):

AirBNB.com
Rent out a room in your home, or your whole home while you are away. Or if you own a cabin or other vacation property that sits vacant most of the year, you can rent it out so that it pays for itself and brings you in a bit of income.

Fluidmarket.com
Rent out your belongings.

Getaround.com
Share your car.

Letgo.com
Sell your unwanted stuff.

Spinlister.com
Rent out your bike, surfboard, skis, snowboard.

Turo.com
Rent out your car.

VRBO.com
Vacation Rentals By Owner, also HomeAway. Similar to AirBNB.

FREELANCE

Maybe you have a particular skill to share. You can set up your own freelancing company in your area of expertise, or find freelance work at these sites:

Fiverr.com
Share a variety of services from computers to consulting.

Flexjobs.com
Jobs that are flexible with your time.

Freelancer.com
Freelance jobs.

SideIncomeJobs.com
This site offers 'flexible-schedule' jobs.

Taskrabbit.com
Offer to share your expertise helping with household tasks
handyman, yard work, furniture assembly, moving services,
cleaning services.

Upwork.com
Share your expertise by freelancing as a writer, designer, coder,
graphic designer...

DRIVE

Are you at an age when you're still driving safely? Perhaps
consider a part time job with a delivery (people and packages)
service.

Postmates.com
Deliver goods and food.

Lyft.com
Be a Lyft driver and take people places.

Uber.com
Be an Uber driver for people who want to "take an Uber".

GIVE YOUR OPINION

Sometimes your opinion pays. The following sites pay for
feedback:

TryMyUI.com

Userlytics.com

Ubertesting.com

WRITE

MAGAZINE ARTICLES

Do you subscribe to magazines in your 'field of passion'? Have you read articles where you've thought – I could have written that! Or have you thought, why do they never provide articles on this? Many magazines accept non-solicited articles. I myself have written – and got paid for – a few articles in trade magazines in my field. If you have some knowledge about your passion to share, go for it!

HOW TO WRITE A BOOK

Do you have a book inside your head, but feel that it's too daunting of a task and that you don't have a large chunk of time?

Start small. If it's a fictional book, publish one short story at a time. If it's a non-fiction book, publish one article at a time. Before you know it, you'll have a book. That's how I got started with the first book I ever published "Rise Above Your Divorce and Land on Your Feet" (under the pseudonym Betty Gordon). I wrote – and published - 4 articles on finances, emotions, organization and the future. And then I realized I had a book. I've published 7 books since then, primarily in my field, but all started out small and all were based on past experiences.

And, again, this is a good time to be in a Mindset Retirement. No longer do you have to search for an agent or a publisher. There are several platforms online where you can publish your own book – for free! The service I use is Amazon's Createspace. It really is as crazily simple as picking your title, picking a cover design template, uploading your word file or pdf and clicking Publish! You are charged nothing for the service. You do not have to pre-pay for any books to be printed (unless you want to order some for yourself – and even then you can order your own books at a significantly lower cost). Every time someone orders your book, it's printed out right then and there (don't ask me how they managed to make printing one book at a time cost effective but they did!), and you get a royalty. It sounds too good to be true. But it's a win-win for the publishing company and for the author. The book you are holding in your hand went through this process. If I can do it, you can too!

GET PAID TO LEARN?

<u>GOING BACK TO SCHOOL</u>

Throughout this book I've been avoiding mentioning going back to school. For most of us at this stage in our lives, we would never recoup the costs. But there is one option if you're academically inclined and have at least a Bachelors degree, here's an idea... Consider going back to school in your specialty area – for a PhD.

It is possible to go straight to a PhD, skipping a Masters or including a Masters, and - get paid to go to school! At the writing of this book my older son and his girlfriend have just started their first year of grad school to get their PhDs, right out of their undergrad program. And – they are each being *PAID* $20,000/yr. by the university. Together they have a household income of $40,000/yr! I have looked into doing the same thing myself – who knows...

How can that be? If you've been to college, or if you've had your own kids in college, you probably know that some undergrad classes are taught by grad students, not the professors. The universities pay these grad students to teach. Many PhD programs require that you teach while you are earning your degree – usually there's a cap, but it can be for 4 to 6 years. Of course, you don't get paid for teaching what a professor is paid, but you get paid to get an education and the university gets cheap labor. It's a win-win.

I also hear you say – there's no way I could pass the GRE (Graduate Records Examinations required by many universities), I haven't taken a test in decades! To that end, I encourage you to sign up to take the test anyway. You may pass, and if you don't, you can study, and take it again. The GRE is just one thing in a checklist of requirements for your application to be accepted. Most likely there is an administrative person who has been charged with making sure the applications are complete before passing them on to the people in the department who make the decisions on acceptance. A minimum score (some universities have different requirements) can be all that is needed to fulfill the requirement and get your application passed on. The GRE is not the only thing taken into account when considering your application. I was once accepted into a prestigious university for undergrad (I didn't end up choosing to go there) and my SAT scores were abysmal. But they take into account your overall GPA, your life experiences, what you can offer the university, and other factors that will make you a good candidate. So if you are interested in funding the next 4 to 6 years of your retirement by this route, I encourage you to at least make the attempt.

It's another option for some people, and who says you can't go back to school at this stage of your life. Then, once you have your PhD you can further fund your retirement - teach or otherwise change the world!

THE NOMADIC LIFE

You might even consider being a nomad. Yes, a nomad. A review of the book "Nomadland: Surviving America in the Twenty-First Century, by Jessica Bruder, in the September 25, 2017 issue of Time Magazine, talks about the "...tens of thousands of Americans whose safety nets were decimated after the 2008 recession..." and how the "...formerly middle-class senior citizens... are now finding work and happiness after selling their homes and buying trailers and RVs, and traveling around the country taking seasonal jobs."

CASH IN YOUR PASSION

These are only a few ideas of how to fund your Mindset Retirement. The main point is to do what YOU are passionate about. Consider – even if you were a multi-millionaire, what would you continue to do in your retirement? Regardless of how you found yourself in this world with no prospect of a Financial Retirement you can still make it financially in your Mindset Retirement.

Chapter 10

Your New Retirement Mindset

*"The moment you doubt whether you can fly,
you cease for ever to be able to do it."*
- J.M. Barrie, Peter Pan

I know that right now it may feel like this phase between now and collecting social security will never end, but remember life is resilient. You are resilient. Focus on what you can control today. What you can control today is your mindset. The rest will follow.

MINDSET MOTIVATIONS

Here's some parting inspirations to see you on your way:

PAST PASSIONS

Can't think what you will do in your new Mindset Retirement? One thing that helped me – look back on your life and ask yourself, what is it that you have enjoyed doing the most, what are you good at, what can you help others do. I'm not necessarily advocating starting your own business, because while that can be productive and lucrative, doing things on speculation can also be risky at this time of your life, but use that information as a foundation for looking for the type of work you might enjoy. You can capitalize on your past strengths and your fundamental character assets and make researched, educated, calculated choices about the opportunities open to you.

HALF FULL

Look at the half full cup, not the half empty cup. As of the writing of this book, the average unemployment rate is hovering around the 4% mark. But, I never hear anyone say "Hooray! The cup is 96% full - 96% of people in this country are employed!" You can be one of those 96% in your Mindset Retirement.

WRONG CUP

Or, as the engineer's joke goes – the cup is the wrong size. Consider that maybe you've got a hold of the wrong cup. Maybe you could be looking elsewhere for the right sized cup to put your passions into. Possibly consider a new passion.

CUPS IN ABUNDANCE

Or, to go one step further – the optimist will say "There is more than one cup!" There is more than one choice available for you out there. You don't just have to do one thing.

THE BEST THING

Instead of dwelling on the worst thing that can happen, as if it's reality already, ask yourself "What's the best thing that can happen?"!

FAKE IT 'TIL YOU MAKE IT

Facial expression and body posture not only depict your inner demeanor, but can create your inner demeanor. Catch a glimpse of yourself in a window or mirror – what is your body posture telling you? I once found myself walking around with my shoulders hunched up around my ears and rolled forwards, and my hair in my face. Are you leaning forward and protecting your heart? Do you wear your hair around your face in order to avoid being seen, or maybe in order to avoid seeing? I decided I was trying to hold myself up (the image came to mind of a person hunched over holding the chains of a playground swing while sitting on it) if you can't hold yourself up, you'll fall. So, instead – even if you don't feel like it at first, "stand up for yourself"; try standing tall, shoulders back, chin up" not slumped and protecting your heart – how do you feel?

HELP WHEN YOU CAN

I have found that people going through a Mindset Retirement don't necessarily feel that they need to be in the top 1% of wealth, or even want to make off with puts of gold.

I am reminded of a joke that I recently came across where a wealthy man was asked to donate to a worthy cause, to which he replied something to the effect that his mother was ill, his brother had just had a house fire, and his neighbors children never seemed to have any new clothes. At that point the charity solicitor felt awful because this man already had so much going on in his life, until the man continued, saying that he wasn't helping out those people out, so why should he help out the charity! In my experience, far too many wealthy people have this miserly attitude. People joke "how do you think they became rich in the first place". It's rather a sad little joke, don't you think.

As well as moral and practical support, I also try to give others financial support. I can't afford to give much, but I give when I can. I have a (albeit small) monthly donation to our local NPR radio station, plus I donate unwanted clothes and household items to community services, and I once did something I've meant to do for many years – I sponsored a child through Save the Children.

Whether you believe it or not right now, at some point you will be living your Mindset Retirement. Once you have your life in order, I encourage you to give back, advocate and/or get involved in helping others in need. I often think that I can never directly pay back the people who have helped me along in my journey, but I can help the next person, who will never be able to repay me either, but will be able to help the next person, and so on and so on. Yes, there will always be people worse off than you, so if you're doing ok then help someone out, and help yourself out by empowering your retirement mindset with this acknowledgement.

LESSONS FROM A ROAD TRIP ON THE EDGE

A good book I recommend is Tim Tyler's "A Passion for the Edge: Living Your Dreams Now". Reading it changed the way I do many things. Interspersed with anecdotes from his solo motorcycle trip across Alaska are insightful and inspirational lessons. Whether or not you are a motorcycle enthusiast (I'm not) Tim Tyler's philosophy on how to 'live your dreams now' is contagious – and, when applied, actually works. While his ideas are not original, the way he presents them makes you sit up and take notice. Although I recommend you read the book yourself for the highest inspiration and personal understanding, here are a few of my favorite lessons of his that have certainly helped me in my life:

> *Plan from the furthest point that you can see, back to where you are now.*
>
> *Most perceived obstacles never happen.*
>
> *The road towards your dream is no more uncertain than any other road you take, so why walk down a road other than one you wish to be on.*
>
> *Be aware of the advice of others; a situation or set of circumstances that applied to them may not apply to you in the same way in your life.*
>
> *Fears about potential dangers only have value at the time of preparation. If you don't hit a pothole, it's not dangerous to you.*
>
> *It's vital to stay in action, continuously accelerate, and modify while in action.*
>
> *And contrary to everything you've heard about diversifying - put all your eggs in one basket – and watch that basket! Alternative plans distract and offer a way out.*

LESSONS FROM MY OWN ROAD TRIP

And here's a little 'road trip' lesson of my own. One day we were driving to the cabin we used to own, and my then 8 year old son asked out of the blue "why do they build roads in the middle of nowhere?" I thought for a minute and then I answered "in order to get from somewhere to somewhere, you have to drive through the middle of nowhere." When you are in the middle of your Mindset Retirement transition it feels like you are in the middle of nowhere. But, you *were* somewhere and you will eventually *be* somewhere. It may not be the retirement you were expecting, but it will be your New Retirement, and it all belongs to you! Focus on what you can control today in order to get somewhere tomorrow.

THE BEST

You will probably come across the naysayers who will tell you that you must do your best to get a full time job, with as many benefits as you can get, for as long as you can keep working. What if you fall ill? What if you have a large unexpected expense? You've got to plan for "*What's the worst that can happen?*"!

You must consider they may be right. It may be true that that route is the best for you. Only you know. But if you are an entrepreneuring, proactive spirit remember to weigh all your options and ask yourself:

What's the BEST that can happen?!

HAPPY RETIREMENT!

No doubt it's tough to find you have to go through your retirement without the financial infrastructure you'd once planned on. A retirement like this is tough both emotionally and financially. And while it may at times feel like the cup is half empty, remember, there are in fact many cups! Let's have one more look at a few of the cups I chose to fill:

- ✓ Designing.

- ✓ Consulting.

- ✓ Tutoring.

- ✓ Teaching an online course.

- ✓ Writing.

I know you can do it! I know you will make it! Many of us make it and you can too with the support and advice from this book, your family, friends and community, and your other resources.

Now make your own list.

✓ _____ (*fill in your own*).

✓ _____ (*fill in your own*).

✓ _____ (*fill in your own*).

✓ _____ (*fill in your own*).

Enjoy your Mindset Retirement!

RESOURCES

It's been said the best step to reaching your goal is finding the right person who can help you. Sometimes that person comes to you personally, sometimes in the form of a book or website.

There are a lot of resources out there if you know where to look for them. The trouble is, when you are first going through your Mindset Retirement, you don't know where to turn. Following is a list of just some of the resources that I've come across that will help you out. These are my suggestions only and certainly are not the only resources available to you. Talk with your lawyer, your financial advisor, and friends. Check out websites for information specific to your state and location. The important thing is to be in action and be your own advocate, because no one is going to do it for you.

I don't endorse any of the following – you have to create your own path – but the these have been very helpful to me:

BOOKS
(Alphabetical by author last name.)

"Women Don't Ask: Negotiation and the Gender Divide" by Linda Babcock and Sara Laschener

"Taking Charge of Your Career" by Nella Barkley

"Happy Beginnings: How I Became My Own Fairy Godmother" by Lorena Bathey

"Texas – Land of the Big Hair (Big Divorce Texas Style!)" by Sonya Bernhardt

"Fearless Living" by Rhonda Britten

"Go Put Your Strengths To Work" by Marcus Buckingham

"Don't Worry, Make Money" by Richard Carlson

"Is Self-Employment for You?" by Paul Casey

"Trust Your Vibes at Work" by Sonia Choquette

"Rules for Renegades" by Christine Comaford-Lynch

"10 Secrets for Success and Inner Peace" by Wayne Dyer

"The 4-Hour Workweek" by Tim Ferriss

"Rise Above Your Divorce and Land on Your FEET: Financially secure; Emotionally stable; Efficiently operating; Tomorrow focused" by Betty Gordon (That's me! My pseudonym necessary a the time of publication.)

"The Heart Speaks" by Mimi Guarneri M.D.

"Suddenly Single: Money Skills for Divorcees and Widows" by Kerry Hannon

"Talent is Not Enough" by Molly Hunter

"The Mindful Way Through Depression" By Kabat-Zinn

"If the Buddha Got Stuck" by Charlotte Kasl, Ph. D.

"Fair Share Divorce for Women" by Kathleen Miller, CFP, MBA

"Women and Money" by Suze Orman

 "Steps to Small Business Start-Up" by Linda Pinson

"The Boomers Guide to Retirement" by Jonathan Pond

"A Passion for the Edge: Living Your Dreams Now" by Tim Tyler

COMPUTER PROGRAMS FOR FINANCES

Home Finance

Kiplinger's Simply Money

Managing Your Money

Microsoft Money

Quicken

Wealthbuilder

FINANCIAL PROFESSIONALS

Consumer Credit Counseling Service
www.cccsatl.org
"A non-profit organization that provides confidential financial
guidance, free consumer credit counseling services, educational
resources and debt management assistance." [David Horowitz.]

Institute of Certified Financial Planners
1-800-282-7526

International Association for Financial Planning (IAFP)
1-800-945-4237
Free Guide: "Consumer Guide to Comprehensive Financial
Planning"

National Association of Personal Financial Advisors
(Fee only)
1-800-366-2732

MAGAZINES

AARP

Entrepreneur

Inc

Money

Success

SUPPORT and SELF-EMPOWERMENT

AA/Al Anon

Landmark Education
(If you do nothing else, do this! In just three days you will have a completely unexpected new outlook on life.)

Weight Watchers

WEBSITES

aarp.org
American Association of Retired Persons (join when you are 50)

AARP.org/jobs

annualcreditreport.com or 877-322-8228
once a year you can ask for a free credit report

bankrate.com
search for best deals on checking and savings accounts, and best credit card rates

businessweek.com/smallbiz

cardweb.com
find best credit card rates

cheapskatemonthly.com
debt-Proof Living

EdX.org
Free courses offered by colleges.

finaid.com

giftcardgranny.com
Buy gift cards to save money on regular purchases (extra AARP discounts in some cases).

housingeducation.org
Homeownership information and education

HomeAdvisor.com
Companies have been vetted and will bid on any size project.

liveoutloud.com
and
wealthdiva.com
Related websites on wealth building.

makemineamillion.com

MicroMasters
Low cost online degrees.

mominventors.com

moneywisewomen.net
Educational Services about finances.

nfcc.org
National Foundation for Credit Counseling recommends reputable credit counseling services.

offices2share.com

outschool.com

patientadvocate.com

peointernational.org

Restaurant.com
Before eating out, look for coupons.

retirement jobs.com

sba.gov/womeninbusiness
suzeorman.com

score.org

vocationvacation.com

wallethub.com
Find 0% credit cards